40 GREAT SCENIC RUNS IN ENGLAND & WALES

Vertebrate Publishing, Sheffield
v-publishing.co.uk

Good Run Guide

40 GREAT SCENIC RUNS IN ENGLAND & WALES

Louise Piears & Andy Bickerstaff

 Published in 2014 by Vertebrate Publishing.
v-publishing.co.uk

ISBN 978-1-906148-90-4

Cover photo: On the Chevin above Otley (run 27). Photo: Ben Winston.
Photography by Louise Piears and Andy Bickerstaff unless otherwise credited.

 Design and production by Jane Beagley.
v-graphics.co.uk

Printed and bound in China.

MIX
Paper from
responsible sources
FSC
www.fsc.org FSC® C016973

Contents

Download PDFs of the *Good Run Guide*
maps from **grg.v-publishing.co.uk**

■ EASY   ■ MODERATE   ■ HARD   ■ EXTREME

Introduction

There are so many amazing places to visit in England and Wales and running is a great way to explore many of them, while at the same time keeping fit. If you are limited on time when visiting an area, or just like to run, even the slowest jogging can get you to spectacular places within a relatively short space of time.

Over the past seven years, while searching out the best routes for the *Good Run Guide* – **goodrunguide.co.uk** – we have found an abundance of interesting places and landmarks combined with beautiful scenery. For this book we have picked out 40 of our favourite runs in England and Wales, each with an awe-inspiring view.

There is a variety of different grades and lengths of routes to choose from, so you can pick your run according to your mood, experience and time available. There are plenty of easy and relatively short runs if you fancy a gentle jog, but we have also included more challenging routes, for those who enjoy a nice tough run. There's nothing more rewarding than taking on a lung bursting ascent and then emerging at the most wonderful view.

If you are visiting a new place on business, want to discover more about an area while on holiday, or just enjoy using your running as a way to explore, we hope that these routes will meet your needs perfectly.

And of course, all of these routes are a reason for visiting somewhere new in itself!

Andy Bickerstaff and Louise Piears

THE LONG SNAKE RUN

PHOTO: JAMES KIRBY

Acknowledgements

First of all we would like to acknowledge the support of Ranelagh Harriers (our current club) and Great Western Runners (Andy's first club), two great communities full of enthusiastic runners and past runners, who have individually and collectively provided support, motivation and friendship over many years. Without them our running experience wouldn't have been the same, and possibly not as lengthy!

We also acknowledge the support of John Piears for being the technical wizard behind the *Good Run Guide* website and also many members of the site for suggestions and help on the best routes and places to run – hopefully you know who you are! On our travels while researching this book we have stayed in numerous cheap chain hotels and a trusty one man tent (Andy), while useful and necessary they don't really warrant an acknowledgement. But, Andy would like to give a special mention to the warm hospitality of Clive and Sue at Thornthwaite Grange Bed and Breakfast near Keswick in the Lakes. Both Clive and Sue are accomplished runners of vast experience and provide the perfect base and information for a running holiday in the Lakes or even a holiday in the Lakes with a little running or walking. Andy would also like to thank Oliver Bratton and his lovely family who put up with him staying at their home near Consett, Durham whilst exploring the area, often with Oliver's guidance and companionship. Thanks of course also go to John Coefield of Vertebrate Publishing for taking this project on and enabling us to share our fantastic runs in print.

How we choose our routes

All of our routes are chosen for their scenic potential, but practicality is taken into account as well. We try and make the routes as simple to follow as possible as we, as runners, don't want to be stopping all the time to check on the route in the same way as a hill walker might do. We also try to avoid too many obstacles which break a run up, such as stiles and gates or overgrown paths, so sometimes the route may miss a slightly more scenic direction, but is taken that way for practicality. However, all of our routes have great views and/or interesting landmarks, some for the whole route and some at various points along the way.

Guide to following the routes

Always allow more time than you expect to run a route for the first time, as you will invariably spend a bit of time checking the map and admiring the views. If you are judging the distance on pace then allow to be slower than your normal pace, especially on the hilly routes where the gradient and terrain can make a considerable difference. Our **flat distance equivalent** can assist you in evaluating how long it will take you to run a route. See below.

Make sure that you keep to the proper paths (most of our runs use well signed footpaths or bridleways). Sometimes you will need to follow indistinct footpaths across fields and on these occasions take note of the direction of the last footpath sign. Of course, don't forget to leave gates as you find them (usually closed).

Remember that the weather, especially recent rain, will make a considerable difference to the underfoot conditions. Although we do try and avoid the muddier paths, routes surveyed at dry times could be quite muddy at others.

Distance, difficulty, hilliness and terrain

Distance

Our routes are measured using GPS and readjusted when necessary using our Google route planner to ensure the best accuracy, so you won't be caught out. The route distances in this book vary from just over 3 miles to just over 10 miles.

Flat distance equivalent

As a lot of the routes are quite hilly we also calculate the **climb rate** and the **flat distance equivalent** to give you a better idea of the effort and time involved. The **flat distance equivalent** is our estimate of the distance you could expect to run **in the same time** on a flat surface.

It is **not** simply an adjustment of the distance for the vertical ascent though, as this adjustment is negligible at typical gradients experienced by runners.

So, for example, if a 5 mile hilly route had a flat distance equivalent of 5.5 miles, you could expect to take as long to run the 5 mile route as you would running 5.5 miles over a flat course.

Climb rate
The climb rate is the **average** number of metres climbed per mile of the run. We calculate this by dividing the total climb for the whole route by the length of the route.

Difficulty
Our routes are rated according to our perceived degree of difficulty: **Easy**, **Moderate**, **Hard** and **Extreme**. These grades take into account the length, the terrain and the hilliness of the run, and are in comparison to the other routes, and other routes you'll find on the Good Run Guide website. Of course this is subjective, as what may be easy for a fell runner, for example, may be extremely hard for a beginner who is used to short, flat runs.

Hilliness
In addition to the overall grade of the run, we have also given a measure of how hilly the run is: **Flat**, **Undulating**, **Hilly**, **Extreme**. This is based on the **climb rate** – those with a **climb rate** under 10 metres are considered **Flat**, 10 to 20 metres are **Undulating**, 20 to 60 metres are **Hilly** and routes of over 60 metres are classed as **Extreme**.

Terrain
We have described the terrain of each run after the route title so you know what to expect, be it lanes, gravel tracks, grass, footpaths or something else.

Directions and accuracy
While every effort has been made to ensure accuracy within the directions in this guide, things do change and we are unable to guarantee that every detail will be correct. Please exercise caution if a direction appears at odds with the route on the ground. A sign/landmark may have been missed so if they don't tally it is usually worth retracing your steps back to the last point to make sure you haven't deviated from the route.

Safety
Headphones
Rather an obvious one to begin with, but we recommend that you don't use headphones on an unfamiliar route. You need to be aware of things around you.

Roads

We try to avoid busy roads if at all possible, but there are some short stretches on a few routes: always use the pavement if there is one. If not, face the oncoming traffic unless there is a blind bend where cars would not see you appearing. Take special care at junctions and when crossing major roads and do not assume that the driver of a car has seen you.

If you can, it's always best to run an unfamiliar route with a companion. If you have to go alone then make sure someone knows where you are going and how long you are likely to be.

Mobile phones

Always carry a mobile phone in case of emergencies, although remember that a signal is not guaranteed.

Footwear

We recommend trail shoes for most of our runs as it can get muddy/slippery and these offer better grip.

Trail surface

Pay attention to the surface you are running on – look out for tripping hazards such as branches and large stones.

Pay attention

Try not to be led astray by scenic/interesting views while you are running. It's always safer to stop and marvel for a while and then carry on, taking care on the path ahead.

Weather

Don't head out in bad weather or when there is a bad forecast, especially on remote/hilly routes as it could quickly turn for the worst and become dangerous. And after all, you won't be able to appreciate the marvellous scenery!

Mountain Rescue

In case of an emergency dial **999** and ask for **Police** and then **Mountain Rescue**. Where possible give a six-figure grid reference of your location or that of the casualty. If you don't have reception where you are, try and attract the help of others around you. The usual distress signal is six short blasts on a whistle every minute. If you don't have a whistle, then shouting may work.

Mountain Rescue by SMS text

Another option in the UK is contacting the emergency services by SMS text – useful if you have a low battery or intermittent signal, but you do need to register your phone first. To register, simply text 'register' to 999 and then follow the instructions in the reply. Do it now – it could save yours or someone else's life. **www.emergencysms.org.uk**

Follow the Countryside Code
Cattle
There have been occasions of people being crushed by cattle, especially when they have dogs with them. If a herd of cattle gives chase then the general advice is to let the dog go as they are generally mobbing the dog, who should be able to avoid them, whereas you may not be able to.

Be safe – plan ahead
Even when going out locally, it's best to get the latest information about where and when you can go; for example, your rights to go onto some areas of open land may be restricted while work is carried out, for safety reasons or during breeding and shooting seasons. Follow advice and local signs, and be prepared for the unexpected.
- Refer to up-to-date maps or guidebooks.
- You're responsible for your own safety and for others in your care, so be prepared for changes in weather and other events.
- There are many organisations offering specific advice on equipment and safety, or contact visitor information centres and libraries for a list of outdoor recreation groups.
- Check weather forecasts before you leave, and don't be afraid to turn back.
- Part of the appeal of the countryside is that you can get away from it all. You may not see anyone for hours and there are many places without clear mobile phone signals, so let someone else know where you're going and when you expect to return.

Leave gates and property as you find them
Please respect the working life of the countryside, as our actions can affect people's livelihoods, our heritage, and the safety and welfare of animals and ourselves.
- A farmer will normally leave a gate closed to keep livestock in, but may sometimes leave it open so they can reach food and water. Leave gates as you find them or follow instructions on signs; if running in a group, make sure the last person knows how to leave the gates.
- In fields where crops are growing, follow the paths wherever possible.
- Use gates and stiles wherever possible – climbing over walls, hedges and fences can damage them and increase the risk of farm animals escaping.
- Our heritage belongs to all of us – be careful not to disturb ruins and historic sites.
- Leave machinery and livestock alone – don't interfere with animals even if you think they're in distress. Try to alert the farmer instead.

Protect plants and animals, and take your litter home
We have a responsibility to protect our countryside now and for future generations, so make sure you don't harm animals, birds, plants or trees.
- Litter and leftover food doesn't just spoil the beauty of the countryside, it can be dangerous to wildlife and farm animals and can spread disease – so take your litter home with you. Dropping litter and dumping rubbish are criminal offences.
- Discover the beauty of the natural environment and take special care not to damage, destroy or remove features such as rocks, plants and trees. They provide homes and food for wildlife, and add to everybody's enjoyment of the countryside.
- Wild animals and farm animals can behave unpredictably if you get too close, especially if they're with their young – so give them plenty of space.
- Fires can be as devastating to wildlife and habitats as they are to people and property – so be careful not to drop a match or smouldering cigarette at any time of the year. Sometimes, controlled fires are used to manage vegetation, particularly on heaths and moors between October and early April, so please check that a fire is not supervised before calling 999.

Keep dogs under close control
The countryside is a great place to exercise dogs, but it is the owner's duty to make sure their dog is not a danger or nuisance to farm animals, wildlife or other people.
- By law, you must control your dog so that it does not disturb or scare farm animals or wildlife. You must keep your dog on a short lead on most areas of open country and common land between 1 March and 31 July, and at all times near farm animals.
- You do not have to put your dog on a lead on public paths as long as it is under close control. But as a general rule, keep your dog on a lead if you cannot rely on its obedience. By law, farmers are entitled to destroy a dog that injures or worries their animals.
- If a farm animal chases you and your dog, it is safer to let your dog off the lead – don't risk getting hurt by trying to protect it.
- Take particular care that your dog doesn't scare sheep and lambs or wander where it might disturb birds that nest on the ground and other wildlife – eggs and young will soon die without protection from their parents.
- Everyone knows how unpleasant dog mess is and it can cause infections – so always clean up after your dog and get rid of the mess responsibly. Also make sure your dog is wormed regularly.

Consider other people

Showing consideration and respect for other people makes the countryside a pleasant environment for everyone – at home, at work and at leisure.

• Busy traffic on small country roads can be unpleasant and dangerous to local people, visitors and wildlife – so slow down and, where possible, leave your vehicle at home, consider sharing lifts and use alternatives such as public transport or cycling. For public transport information, phone Traveline on 0871 200 2233.

• Respect the needs of local people – for example, don't block gateways, driveways or other entry points with your vehicle.

• By law, cyclists must give way to walkers and horse riders on bridleways.

• Keep out of the way when farm animals are being gathered or moved and follow directions from the farmer.

• Support the rural economy – for example, buy your supplies from local shops.

Essential kit

This depends upon the time of year and the difficulty and extreme nature of the route. We do recommend you carry a mobile phone and a small first aid kit, and wear trainers with good grip – trail shoes. In some of the more lonely off-road routes, we recommend carrying a map and compass (and know how to use them), waterproof clothing, whistle and snack bar.

Planning your run

Decide on the route according to your mood/ability/where you want to visit, and the time of year and weather forecast. Always allow more time than you think you'll need. Study all the details first and how to get to the start and don't forget to take your trail shoes, clothes that you are happy to get muddy in, the map of course, fluid if you think you will need it, some change for a car park/snack afterwards, dry warm clothes and other shoes for after the run. A GPS is always useful if you have one but it is not essential. If you are running with your dog then don't forget the lead as you may be running through fields with livestock. Most of all, have fun!

Download PDFs of the *Good Run Guide* maps from **grg.v-publishing.co.uk**

Southern
England
&Wales

Our routes in this section cover a variety of different landscapes and views, from the cityscape of London to the rolling South Downs, to spectacular coastal routes. Some feature well known iconic views and others offer lesser-known vistas, but they all have one thing in common: the 'wow' factor.

CLASSIC RICHMOND

PHOTO: JON PURCELL

SOUTHERN ENGLAND & WALES

1 THE LONG SNAKE RUN 2 ROLLERCOASTER RUN 3 NORTH CORNISH COVES 4 THE LONG SNAKE RUN 5 RHOSSILI BAY RAMBLE

6 NORTH CORNISH COVES 7 BRISTOL'S AVON GORGE 8 CLASSIC RICHMOND 9 GOLDEN CAP CHALLENGE 10 LANDMARK THAMES TROT PHOTO: SHUTTERSTOCK
11 ROLLERCOASTER RUN

01 North Cornish Coves

A coastal route passing lovely Cornish coves

Distance: **7.32 miles/11.78 km** | Hilly | **HARD**

Flat equiv.: **7.84 miles/12.61 km** | Climb rate: **19m/mile**

Terrain: **Coastal paths and country lanes**

Parking: **Trevone Bay car park, off Trevone Road, Trevone**

Post code: **PL28 8QY** | Grid Ref: **SW 891759**

Start: **On Coast Path, heading towards Roundhole Point**

This is a quite tough yet very satisfying run around Stepper Point, passing numerous beautiful Cornish coves, with great views throughout.

The run starts from Trevone Bay and follows the South West Coast Path towards Padstow and then returns along pretty footpaths and very quiet country lanes. This is not a route to take at too fast a pace – be sure to enjoy the views and take care to avoid all the walkers! There are several points of interest, including The Daymark, a stone tower at Stepper Point which can be seen for much of the run, and it's also worth making a short diversion to peer down Round Hole, an impressive blowhole formed by a collapsed sea cave.

Facilities and safety

There is a car park next to Trevone Bay, very near to the start of the Coast Path, although it can get very busy in the summer holidays. Here you will find toilets and a cafe. Being the Coast Path, it is fairly stony in places and there are some steep downhills to negotiate, so take great care. Also, this area is popular with walkers so allow plenty of time. Some of the stiles may be difficult to negotiate for large dogs as the gaps are small. Trail shoes are recommended.

Interesting information

The Daymark stone tower stands at 40 feet high and 240 feet above sea level. Apparently it is visible from up to 30 miles away which explains why it can be seen for much of the route and is a handy navigation check. It was built in 1832 as a visual guide to the harbour entrance for ships, but presumably was more useful during daylight as it never actually housed any sort of beacon. In 2002 the NCI (National Coastwatch Institution) Lookout Station was built nearby.

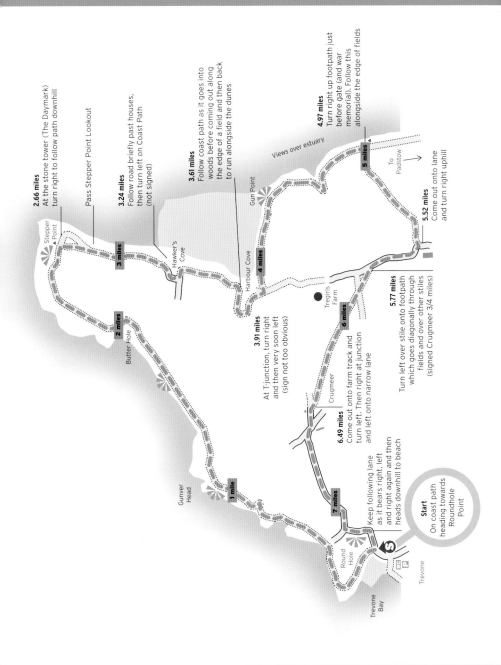

2.66 miles
At the stone tower (The Daymark) turn right to follow path downhill

Pass Stepper Point Lookout

3.24 miles
Follow road briefly past houses, then turn left on Coast Path (not signed)

3.61 miles
Follow coast path as it goes into woods before coming out along the edge of a field and then back to run alongside the dunes

4.97 miles
Turn right up footpath just before gate (and war memorial). Follow this alongside the edge of fields

Views over estuary

Stepper Point

3 miles

Hawker's Cove

Gun Point

Harbour Cove

4 miles

5 miles

To Padstow →

5.52 miles
Come out onto lane and turn right uphill

Butter Hole

2 miles

3.91 miles
At T-junction, turn right and then very soon left (sign not too obvious)

Tregirls Farm

6 miles

5.77 miles
Turn left over stile onto footpath which goes diagonally through fields and over other stiles (signed Crugmeer 3/4 miles)

Crugmeer

Gunver Head

1 mile

6.49 miles
Come out onto farm track and turn left. Then right at junction and left onto narrow lane

7 miles

Keep following lane as it bears right, left and right again and then heads downhill to beach

Start
On coast path heading towards Roundhole Point

Round Hole

Trevone

Trevone Bay

02 The River Yealm Estuary

Stunning views from the South West Coast Path

Distance: **4.80 miles/7.72 km** | Hilly | **MODERATE**

Flat equiv.: **5.18 miles/8.33 km** | Climb rate: **21m/mile**

Terrain: **Footpaths, coastal track and road**

Parking: **Coach Road car park, Noss Mayo**

Post code: **PL8 1EG** | Grid Ref: **SX 547474**

Start: **Cross road from CP, left onto Foundry Lane, and turn R at house 4 on steep path uphill**

A bracing run around the headland from the attractive Devon village of Noss Mayo, with great views over the English Channel and the River Yealm estuary.

A stiff climb is rewarded with spectacular views over the rugged coastline as the route follows the South West Coast Path around the headland, before a gradual downhill along a tree lined track running alongside the sheltered mouth of the River Yealm. Take the time to stop and admire the myriad of boats bobbing in the estuary, from fishing boats to impressive yachts. A good viewpoint is from the interesting ferry point.

Facilities and safety

There is a free car park at Noss Mayo and also a National Trust car park on route. The Ship Inn is near the start in quaint Noss Mayo, but there are no shops. Public toilets are near the Ship Inn. Some of the paths taken can be fairly stony and of course it can get very blustery along the Coast Path.

Interesting information

The Warren was originally managed for the propagation of rabbits, and Warren Cottage was built to house the warrener who farmed the rabbits. The South West Coast Path itself runs for 630 miles from Minehead in Somerset to Poole in Dorset. The level path around the headland was originally cut out of the rock by Lord Revelstoke, of the Baring banking family, who wanted a drive for horse and carriages. Hence its name – the Revelstoke Drive. He employed a team of men to do the work so he could show off his (now demolished) manor to his friends.

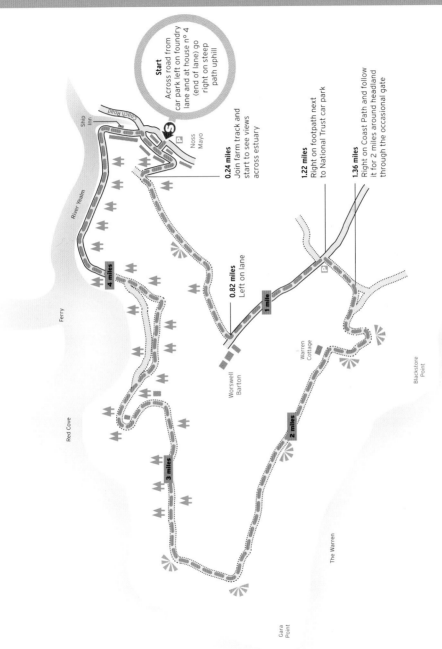

Start
Across road from car park left on foundry lane and at house n° 4 (end of lane) go right on steep path uphill

0.24 miles
Join farm track and start to see views across estuary

1.22 miles
Right on footpath next to National Trust car park

1.36 miles
Right on Coast Path and follow it for 2 miles around headland through the occasional gate

0.82 miles
Left on lane

Ship Inn

Coach Road

Noss Mayo

River Yealm

Ferry

Red Cove

4 miles

1 mile

Worswell Barton

Warren Cottage

2 miles

3 miles

Blackstore Point

The Warren

Gara Point

03 Golden Cap Challenge

A challenging run with spectacular coastal views

Distance: **4.91 miles/7.90 km** | Hilly | **HARD**

Flat equiv.: **5.77 miles/9.28 km** | Climb rate: **47m/mile**

Terrain: **Grassy paths, trails and country lane**

Parking: **Car park, Stonebarrow Lane, Charmouth**

Post code: **DT6 6SD** | Grid Ref: **SY 381932**

Start: **Fingerpost behind car park, signed** *Golden Cap/Coast Path*

This is a spectacular but challenging run which follows the South West Coast Path to the top of Dorset's Golden Cap. Marvellous views more than make up for the punishing climb before a pleasant return route along grassy fields, footpaths and quiet country lanes.

Starting with a gentle downhill run to meet the Coast Path, the serious climb (often with steps) begins at about 1.75 miles out. If you can make it all the way to the lung-busting top without pausing for too long then you will certainly impress the walkers you will undoubtedly meet coming the other way. Take time at the top to appreciate the wonderful views to the west and the east along the south coast. The return is generally pleasant, with a little bit of uphill thrown in towards the end.

Facilities and safety

There is a National Trust car park at the start and a small visitor centre which is open at peak times. Some of the paths are stony so take care, and a short part of the Coast Path is within a few feet of the edge of the cliff so be prepared for this. This route starts a few miles from Charmouth, a small seaside town with shops, cafes and a beach very popular with fossil hunters. Trail shoes are recommended.

Interesting information

At 188m high Golden Cap is the tallest cliff along the south coast and is part of the West Dorset Heritage Coast. The name comes from the distinctive cap of gold coloured sand which can be seen on the cliff face. The cliff face was formed in the last 10,000 years and the top of Golden Cap is a preserved land surface some 50 million years old.

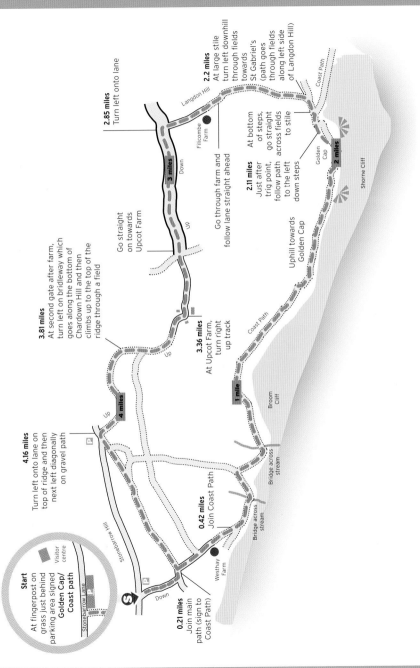

Start
At fingerpost on grass just behind parking area signed **Golden Cap/ Coast path**

Visitor centre

Stonebarrow Lane

0.21 miles
Join main path (sign to Coast Path)

Down

Westhay Farm

0.42 miles
Join Coast Path

Stonebarrow Hill

Bridge across stream

Bridge across stream

Broom Cliff

1 mile

Coast Path

3.36 miles
At Upcot Farm, turn right up track

Up

4 miles

Up

4.16 miles
Turn left onto lane on top of ridge and then next left diagonally on gravel path

3.81 miles
At second gate after farm, turn left on bridleway which goes along the bottom of Chardown Hill and then climbs up to the top of the ridge through a field

Go straight on towards Upcot Farm

Up

3 miles

Down

Go through farm and follow lane straight ahead

2.85 miles
Turn left onto lane

Langdon Hill

Filicombe Farm

Uphill towards Golden Cap

2.11 miles
Just after trig point, follow path to the left down steps

At bottom of steps, go straight across fields to stile

Golden Cap

2 miles

Coast Path

2.2 miles
At large stile turn left downhill through fields towards St Gabriel's (path goes through fields along left side of Langdon Hill)

Coast Path

Shorne Cliff

04 Osmington White Horse

Cross country running with beautiful views over Weymouth Bay

Distance: **4.66 miles/7.50 km** | **Hilly** | **HARD**

Flat equiv.: **5.13 miles/8.25 km** | Climb rate: **27m/mile**

Terrain: **Mostly footpaths and cross country with a short road section**

Parking: **Near village pond and The Springhead pub, Sutton Poyntz**

Post code: **DT3 6LW** | Grid Ref: **SY 706837**

Start: **Up the road from The Springhead pub**

A lovely run that circles the Osmington White Horse, overlooking Weymouth Bay. There is one fairly hard climb but the views over the bay and the Isle of Portland are well worth the effort.

Starting next to The Springhead pub (useful for post-run refuelling) in pretty Sutton Poyntz, the route goes first across fields with grazing livestock and then runs parallel to the White Horse, which can be clearly seen up on Osmington Hill to the left. On reaching the outskirts of Osmington, the climb gradually begins onto the top of the hill from where there are spectacular views and a pleasant hilltop run. Return via grassy fields and finish at the quaint village duck pond, or more likely in The Springhead.

Facilities and safety

Parking is available near the village pond and The Springhead pub. The path up the hill is fairly stony and some of the footpaths can be a little muddy at times, especially through the fields. Keep dogs on leads in some of the fields as there is likely to be grazing livestock. Trail shoes are recommended.

Interesting information

The white horse and rider were cut into the hillside in 1808 to commemorate the royal visits to nearby Weymouth by King George III and the prosperity they brought. Mr Wood, the local book seller, directed the construction at the expense and request of John Ranier, brother of Admiral Nelson. The horse was restored in 2010 with the help of local organisations and individuals and a grant from Natural England.

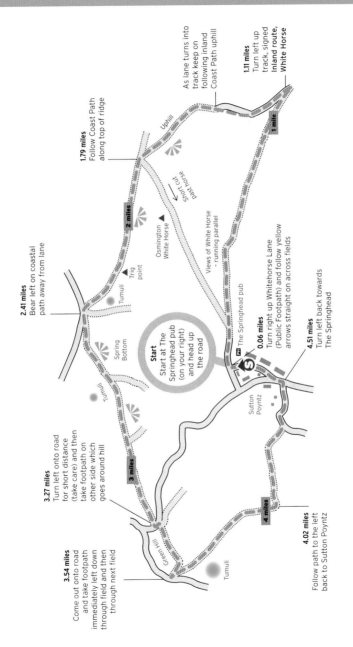

As lane turns into track keep on following inland Coast Path uphill

1.11 miles
Turn left up track, signed Inland route, White Horse

1 mile

Uphill

1.79 miles
Follow Coast Path along top of ridge

Short cut past horse

Osmington White Horse ◄

Views of White Horse - running parallel

2 miles

2.41 miles
Bear left on coastal path away from lane

▲ Trig point

Tumuli

Spring Bottom

Tumuli

Start
Start at The Springhead pub (on your right) and head up the road

🚇 The Springhead pub

0.06 miles
Turn right up Whitehorse Lane (Public Footpath) and follow yellow arrows straight on across fields

4.51 miles
Turn left back towards The Springhead

Sutton Poyntz

3.27 miles
Turn left onto road for short distance (take care) and then take footpath on other side which goes around hill

3 miles

3.54 miles
Come out onto road and take footpath immediately left down through field and then through next field

Green Hill

Tumuli

4 miles

Tumuli

4.02 miles
Follow path to the left back to Sutton Poyntz

05 West Wight Views

A fascinating route taking in many iconic views

Distance: **4.65 miles/7.48 km** | Hilly | **HARD**	
Flat equiv.: **5.50 miles/8.85 km** | Climb rate: **48m/mile**	
Terrain: **Road, trails and grassy downs**	
Parking: **Highdown Lane car park**	
Post code: **PO39 OHY** | Grid Ref: **SZ 325826**	
Start: **Follow lane north from car park**	

A bracing run which takes in many iconic Isle of Wight views including The Needles, the colourful sands of Alum Bay and the south coast of England from Tennyson Down.
 There is a fairly short stretch on quiet lanes and then a steep climb up to Headon Warren, covered with glorious purple heather in the summer months, then a descent to pass the pleasure park, followed by another challenging climb up onto Tennyson Down. The finale is the long grassy run along the top of the Down towards the Tennyson Monument.

Facilities and safety

There is a free car park at the start of the route; if this is full then find a convenient space further along the road. Some of the paths can be stony and/or muddy on occasions, so take care. The path back down to the car park is steep and can be slippery so take special care here. Both Headon Warren and Tennyson Down overlook the coast so it is often very blustery. Trail shoes are recommended. It's also worth noting that Alum Bay is a good place for a family outing with its coloured sands, boat trips, glass making, chair lift and other attractions.

Interesting information

The white chalk cliffs on the southwest coast of the Isle of Wight reach their highest point at 147 metres above sea level at Tennyson Down, re-named after the poet Laureate Lord Alfred Tennyson who lived at nearby Farringford House for nearly 40 years and liked to walk on the Downs.
 The Bronze Age barrow that you will pass on the top of Headon Warren dates back about 3,500 years and is thought to be the burial place of a local chieftain. The mound is likely to be one of those excavated under the orders of Henry III's charter of 1237 which required that barrows be dug in search of treasure for the royal coffers.

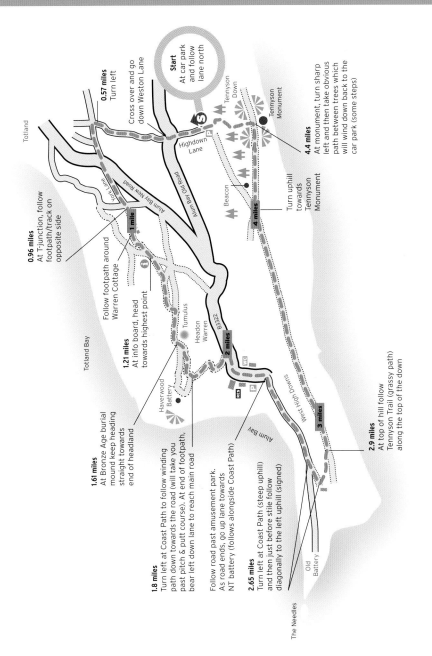

Start
At car park and follow lane north

0.57 miles
Turn left

Cross over and go down Weston Lane

Tennyson Down

Tennyson Monument

4.4 miles
At monument, turn sharp left and then take obvious path between trees which will wind down back to the car park (some steps)

Highdown Lane

Totland

0.96 miles
At T-junction, follow footpath/track on opposite side

York Lane

Alum Bay New Road

Alum Bay Old Road

Beacon

Turn uphill towards Tennyson Monument

4 miles

Totland Bay

Follow footpath around Warren Cottage

1 mile

1.21 miles
At info board, head towards highest point

Tumulus

Headon Warren

B3322

2 miles

WC

1.61 miles
At Bronze Age burial mound keep heading straight towards end of headland

Haverwood Battery

West High Downs

3 miles

2.9 miles
At top of hill follow Tennyson Trail (grassy path) along the top of the down

1.8 miles
Turn left at Coast Path to follow winding path down towards the road (will take you past pitch & putt course). At end of footpath, bear left down lane to reach main road

Follow road past amusement park. As road ends, go up lane towards NT battery (follows alongside Coast Path)

2.65 miles
Turn left at Coast Path (steep uphill) and then just before stile follow diagonally to the left uphill (signed)

Alum Bay

Old Battery

The Needles

06 The Long Snake Run

A peaceful and varied run over the beautiful South Downs

Distance: **9.42 miles/15.16 km** | **Hilly** | **HARD**

Flat equiv.: **10.45 miles/16.81 km** | Climb rate: **29m/mile**

Terrain: **Tracks and footpaths**

Parking: **Car park on Falmer Road, Woodingdean, Brighton**

Post code: **BN2 6NT** | Grid Ref: **TQ 356063**

Start: **At metal gate, on right-hand of two large tracks**

This fairly long run takes a scenic and challenging route over the South Downs near Brighton. With a peaceful, away-from-it-all feel, the only things you'll encounter, apart from the occasional walker and farmer, are likely to be large numbers of sheep roaming over the Downs.

The route is mostly on well-drained trails, with a short section of very quiet tarmac lane, and at infrequent intervals there are gates to negotiate. There are marvellous views all along the route and there is enough variety to keep the interest up throughout. The final gradual climb up *The Snake* is either wonderfully challenging or just challenging depending on your point of view, and how tired you feel by the time you reach it.

Facilities and safety

There is a free car park at the start just off Falmer Road (B2123), immediately north of Woodingdean. Although the trails are generally well drained be prepared for mud in places, and some of the paths are stony. This is sheep country so if running with a dog take a lead. Trail shoes are recommended.

Interesting information

This run takes in part of the route of the Jog Shop Jog 20 mile race, which also takes in local features such as The Snake, a 1.75 miles twisty climb, and Death Valley, the naming of which will be obvious on a hot day! Part of the route takes in the South Downs Way, which follows the old routes and droveways along the chalk escarpment and ridges of the South Downs for 160km.

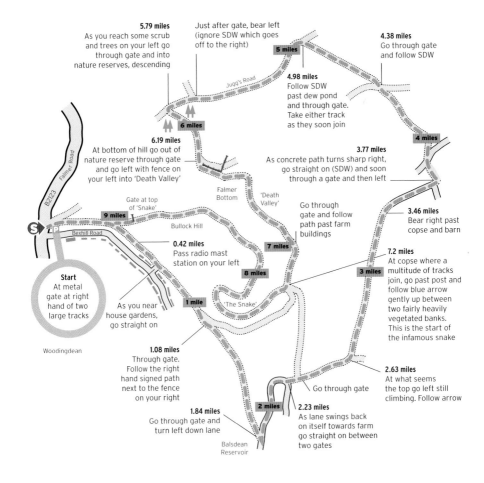

5.79 miles
As you reach some scrub and trees on your left go through gate and into nature reserves, descending

Just after gate, bear left (ignore SDW which goes off to the right)

5 miles

4.38 miles
Go through gate and follow SDW

Jugg's Road

4.98 miles
Follow SDW past dew pond and through gate. Take either track as they soon join

6 miles

6.19 miles
At bottom of hill go out of nature reserve through gate and go left with fence on your left into 'Death Valley'

4 miles

3.77 miles
As concrete path turns sharp right, go straight on (SDW) and soon through a gate and then left

Falmer Bottom

'Death Valley'

Go through gate and follow path past farm buildings

3.46 miles
Bear right past copse and barn

Falmer Road

B2123

Gate at top of 'Snake'

9 miles

Bullock Hill

Bexhill Road

S **P**

0.42 miles
Pass radio mast station on your left

7 miles

7.2 miles
At copse where a multitude of tracks join, go past post and follow blue arrow gently up between two fairly heavily vegetated banks. This is the start of the infamous snake

3 miles

8 miles

Start
At metal gate at right hand of two large tracks

As you near house gardens, go straight on

1 mile

'The Snake'

Woodingdean

1.08 miles
Through gate. Follow the right hand signed path next to the fence on your right

2.63 miles
At what seems the top go left still climbing. Follow arrow

Go through gate

1.84 miles
Go through gate and turn left down lane

2 miles

2.23 miles
As lane swings back on itself towards farm go straight on between two gates

Balsdean Reservoir

THE LONG SNAKE RUN

PHOTO: JAMES KIRBY

07 **Rollercoaster Run**

An enjoyable rollercoaster of a run with spectacular views

Distance: **6.15 miles/9.89 km** | Hilly | **HARD**

Flat equiv.: **6.80 miles/10.94 km** | Climb rate: **28m/mile**

Terrain: **Trails, country lane and grassy headland path**

Parking: **Seven Sisters Visitor Centre car parks, Exceat**

Post code: **BN25 4AD** | Grid Ref: **TV 519995**

Start: **South Downs Way north from Seven Sisters Visitor Centre**

A short challenging blast of a hill right at the beginning sets the tone for this route – don't forget to look back from the top at the spectacular view over Cuckmere Haven.
There then follows a twisty-turny section along the edge of Friston Forest. The real rollercoaster experience comes on the return as you climb up and then descend with rather more speed down four of the Seven Sisters in turn. This is a lovely grassy section of coastline with views as far as the eye can see from the white chalk clifftops.

Facilities and safety

There are two car parks to choose from at the start, plus a visitor centre, cafe and toilets. The path through the forest can become muddy at times so trail shoes are recommended. Also, take obvious care next to the ever-eroding cliff edges, although there are wide grassy areas so there is no need to run right next to the edge! Not surprisingly, it can be blustery on top of the cliffs. This is sheep country so dogs need to be kept under control.

Interesting information

The Seven Sisters cliffs – so named as they are believed to look like nuns with their white habits over their heads – are made of chalk that formed where the South Downs meet the sea. The cliffs are receding on average at about 30-40 centimetres each year. The process is intermittent with major falls occurring after heavy rain or rough seas, often two or three times a year. Where these falls occur the fallen chalk protects the base of the cliffs from the sea and usually there are no further falls in the same places for eight or nine years until the sea undercuts the cliffs again.

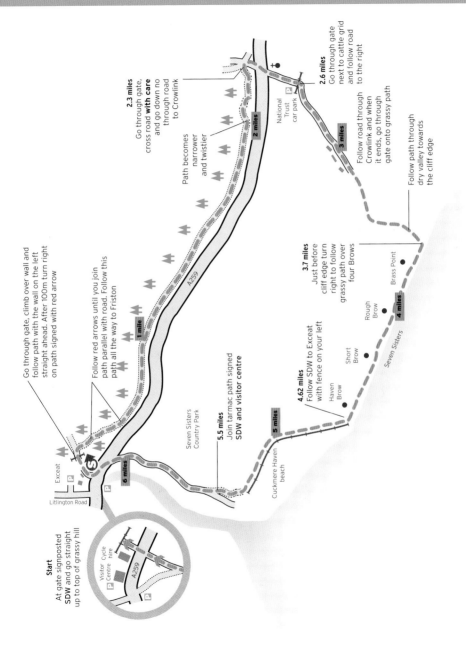

Start
At gate signposted
SDW and go straight
up to top of grassy hill

Go through gate, climb over wall and
follow path with the wall on the left
straight ahead. After 100m turn right
on path signed with red arrow

Follow red arrows until you join
path parallel with road. Follow this
path all the way to Friston

2.3 miles
Go through gate,
cross road **with care**
and go down no
through road
to Crowlink

Path becomes
narrower
and twistier

2.6 miles
Go through gate,
next to cattle grid
and follow road
to the right

3 miles
Follow road through
Crowlink and when
it ends, go through
gate onto grassy path

Follow path through
dry valley towards
the cliff edge

3.7 miles
Just before
cliff edge turn
right to follow
grassy path over
four Brows

Brass Point

Rough
Brow

Short
Brow

Haven
Brow

Seven Sisters

4.62 miles
Follow SDW to Exceat
with fence on your left

5.5 miles
Join tarmac path signed
SDW and **visitor centre**

Seven Sisters
Country Park

Cuckmere Haven
beach

National
Trust
car park

A259

1 mile

2 miles

4 miles

5 miles

6 miles

3 miles

Exceat

Litlington Road

Visitor Cycle
Centre hire

A259

08 Landmark Thames Trot

Gentle and flat, passing many iconic London Landmarks

Distance: **4.72 miles/7.59 km** | **Flat** | EASY

Flat equiv.: **4.86 miles/7.82 km** | Climb rate: **8m/mile**

Terrain: **Pavement and tarmac**

Parking: **N/A. Take Underground to Embankment Station, or train to Charing Cross**

Post code: **WC2N 6NU** | Grid Ref: **TQ 304803**

Start: **Victoria Embankment next to Hungerford railway bridge**

History abounds on this classic run along the Embankment up to and over Tower Bridge and then back along the South Bank.

Running past so many iconic sites brings to mind how important the Thames has been to the history of London over the centuries. This is certainly not a run to blast along; allow plenty of time to jog by and appreciate all the landmarks along the way, and those amazing views on the skyline. The Thames Path is easy to follow and skirts the river with the occasional diversion over bridges and through arches. This run can be even more spectacular after dark with impressive lighting on many of the landmarks, but it can get even busier too, so take extra care.

Facilities and safety

All the facilities you would expect in London are along the route. There are mostly wide pavements to jog along, but of course it can be thronging with workers and sightseers, so be prepared to make way for others criss-crossing your path and occasionally blocking the way.

Interesting information

There are so many sights to see and the old mingles with the new. The most obvious include The Tower, The Shard, Tower Bridge, the Globe Theatre, the National Theatre and the Tate Modern. Tower Bridge still regularly lifts for vessels with superstructure or masts of over 30 feet tall and times are published on the Tower Bridge website. Keep a look out for lesser-known buildings too including the atmospheric Anchor pub on Bankside, from where the diarist Samuel Pepys witnessed the Great Fire of London.

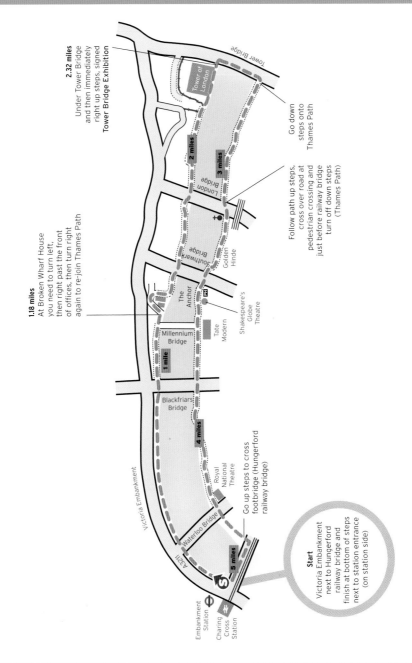

2.32 miles
Under Tower Bridge
and then immediately
right up steps, signed
Tower Bridge Exhibition

Go down
steps onto
Thames Path

1.18 miles
At Broken Wharf House
you need to turn left,
then right past the front
of offices, then turn right
again to re-join Thames Path

Follow path up steps,
cross over road at
pedestrian crossing and
just before railway bridge
turn off down steps
(Thames Path)

Go up steps to cross
footbridge (Hungerford
railway bridge)

Start
Victoria Embankment
next to Hungerford
railway bridge and
finish at bottom of steps
next to station entrance
(on station side)

Tower Bridge

Tower of London

London Bridge

Southwark Bridge

Golden Hinde

The Anchor

Shakespeare's Globe Theatre

Tate Modern

Millennium Bridge

Blackfriars Bridge

Royal National Theatre

Waterloo Bridge

Victoria Embankment

A321

Embankment Station

Charing Cross Station

2 miles
3 miles
1 mile
4 miles
5 miles

09 Classic Richmond

An undulating route through the ever popular Richmond Park

Distance: **7.60 miles/12.22 km** | Undulating | **MODERATE**

Flat equiv.: **7.98 miles/12.83 km** | Climb rate: **13m/mile**

Terrain: **Trail, cross country and road**

Parking: **Roehampton Gate car park**

Post code: **SW15 5JY** | Grid Ref: **TQ 212742**

Start: **South on cycle track**

Although less than 10 miles from the centre of London, Richmond Park is a glorious oasis for running and can seem a world away from the hustle and bustle of city life.
 This run takes in lovely views from the park itself and is extended to include the iconic view from Richmond Hill overlooking the River Thames. Don't forget to check out the views from the 2.5 to 3 mile mark, where many London landmarks can be clearly seen on a good day.

Facilities and safety

Parking is free at the large Roehampton Gate car park where there is a cycle hire shop, a refreshment kiosk and toilets. Some of the run is on tarmac and a short bit on pavement next to a busy road. Take care when crossing the roads in the park and outside. The rest of the run is on a good cycle track with some cross country. Dogs are allowed but take care as deer roam freely. The path next to the Thames is liable to flooding, but it is possible to run through the fields on the other side of the wall to reach River Lane. Trail shoes are recommended.

Interesting information

Richmond Park is the largest open space in London with nearly 1,000 hectares open to the public. It has been designated a Site of Special Scientific Interest and is a National Nature Reserve. There is plenty of wildlife in the park including around 650 red and fallow deer that are allowed to roam freely. The view from the terrace on Richmond Hill is an iconic view that has been painted frequently by artists and described by poets over the centuries.

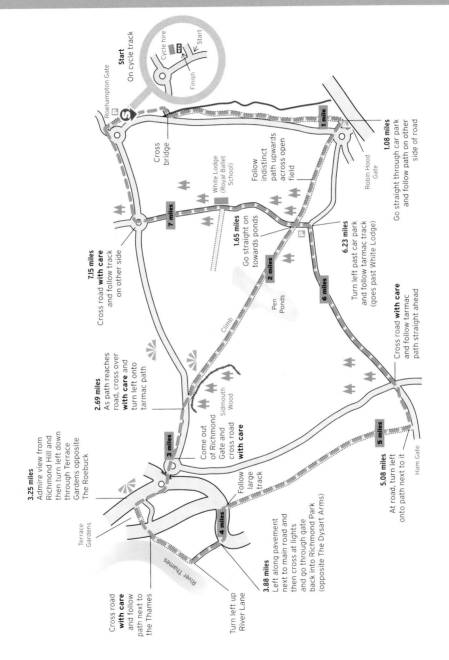

Start
On cycle track

Roehampton Gate

Cycle hire

Start

Finish

Cross
bridge

White Lodge
(Royal Ballet
School)

Follow
indistinct
path upwards
across open
field

1.08 miles
Go straight through car park
and follow path on other
side of road

Robin Hood
Gate

7 miles

7.15 miles
Cross road **with care**
and follow track
on other side

1.65 miles
Go straight on
towards ponds

2 miles

Pen
Ponds

6.23 miles
Turn left past car park
and follow tarmac track
(goes past White Lodge)

6 miles

Climb

Cross road **with care**
and follow tarmac
path straight ahead

2.69 miles
As path reaches
road, cross over
with care and
turn left onto
tarmac path

Sidmouth
Wood

3.25 miles
Admire view from
Richmond Hill and
then turn left down
through Terrace
Gardens opposite
The Roebuck

Come out
of Richmond
Gate and
cross road
with care

3 miles

Follow
large
track

4 miles

5 miles

Ham Gate

5.08 miles
At road, turn left
onto path next to it

Terrace
Gardens

Cross road
with care
and follow
path next to
the Thames

River Thames

Turn left up
River Lane

3.88 miles
Left along pavement
next to main road and
then cross at lights
and go through gate
back into Richmond Park
(opposite The Dysart Arms)

1 mile

CLASSIC RICHMOND

10 Great Park Explorer

A long and interesting run passing many historical features

Distance: **10.70 miles/17.22 km** | **Flat** | **MODERATE**

Flat equiv.: **11.06 miles/17.79 km** | Climb rate: **9m/mile**

Terrain: **Gravel paths, some cross country running and quiet roads**

Parking: **Free parking outside Cheesman's Gate/paid parking in car park**

Post code: **TW20 0HN** | Grid Ref: **SU 982699**

Start: **Cheesman's Gate**

This run explores much of Windsor Great park, a Royal Park of approximately 4,800 acres, passing by plenty of the well-known features, but also taking in some quieter parts, such as Bears Rails, a woodland which is currently being restored to how it would have looked 1,100 years ago.

You will run by the man-made, but beautiful, Virginia Water Lake complete with its own waterfall, The Cascade. Then there is an opportunity to stride out along a tarmac, mostly traffic free road to reach the Copper Horse. A short run along the Long Walk with iconic views of Windsor Castle follows, before a return through the wooded deer park and a final run up Rhododendron Drive and past the Obelisk.

Facilities and safety

There is free parking outside Cheesman's Gate or, if it's full, there is paid parking in the nearby car park. There are toilets and a restaurant in The Savill Garden and next to Virginia Water Lake. Note that the park can be very busy with families and dogs during nice weather, and in certain parts, including the deer park, dogs should be kept on leads. The surface is mainly tarmac or gravel, but there's also some grassland that can get muddy at times. Trail shoes are recommended.

Interesting information

There are so many things to see during this run, so take your time to check out the various information boards. Look out for the figures on the 100-foot high totem pole topped by 'Man with Large Hat', this simple description is worth a chuckle. Something not generally known is that the 1908 Olympic Marathon started on the Long Walk and ended at The Royal Box in the Olympic Stadium and so was fixed at 42.195km (26.2 miles). This in turn, became the official marathon disctance from the 1924 Games onwards.

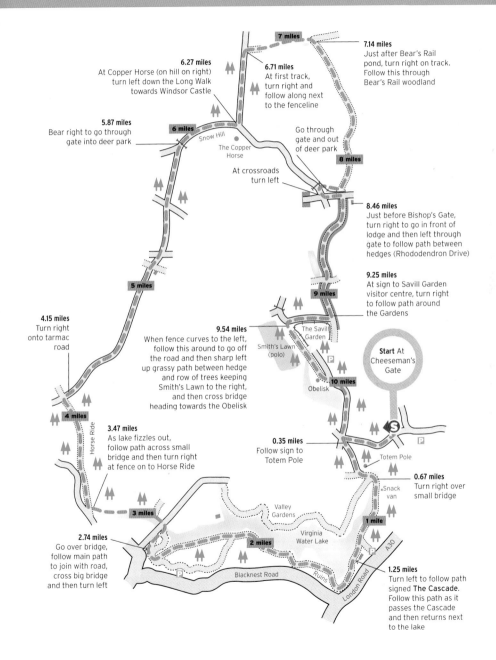

7 miles

7.14 miles
Just after Bear's Rail
pond, turn right on track.
Follow this through
Bear's Rail woodland

6.27 miles
At Copper Horse (on hill on right)
turn left down the Long Walk
towards Windsor Castle

6.71 miles
At first track,
turn right and
follow along next
to the fenceline

5.87 miles
Bear right to go through
gate into deer park

6 miles
Snow Hill

The Copper
Horse

Go through
gate and out
of deer park

8 miles

At crossroads
turn left

8.46 miles
Just before Bishop's Gate,
turn right to go in front of
lodge and then left through
gate to follow path between
hedges (Rhododendron Drive)

5 miles

9.25 miles
At sign to Savill Garden
visitor centre, turn right
to follow path around
the Gardens

9 miles

4.15 miles
Turn right
onto tarmac
road

9.54 miles
When fence curves to the left,
follow this around to go off
the road and then sharp left
up grassy path between hedge
and row of trees keeping
Smith's Lawn to the right,
and then cross bridge
heading towards the Obelisk

The Savill
Garden

Smith's Lawn
(polo)

P

Start At
Cheeseman's
Gate

4 miles

Horse Ride

Obelisk

10 miles

S

P

3.47 miles
As lake fizzles out,
follow path across small
bridge and then turn right
at fence on to Horse Ride

0.35 miles
Follow sign to
Totem Pole

Totem Pole

0.67 miles
Turn right over
small bridge

3 miles

Snack
van

1 mile

Valley
Gardens

Virginia
Water Lake

2.74 miles
Go over bridge,
follow main path
to join with road,
cross big bridge
and then turn left

P

2 miles

Ruins

A30

Blacknest Road

London Road

1.25 miles
Turn left to follow path
signed **The Cascade**.
Follow this path as it
passes the Cascade
and then returns next
to the lake

GREAT PARK EXPLORER

11 Gibbet Gallop

Lovely countryside running with bracing views from the ridge

Distance: **4.64 miles/7.46 km** | Hilly | **HARD**

Flat equiv.: **5.19 miles/8.35 km** | Climb rate: **32m/mile**

Terrain: **Wide tracks, trail and a short bit of quiet road**

Parking: **Free car park near Combe Gibbet**

Post code: **RG17 9EL** | Grid Ref: **SU 366622**

Start: **Across road from car park heading towards the gibbet**

We almost named this route Grisly Gibbet, yet that would have been misleading as it is actually an enjoyable run which follows footpaths, trails and tracks through the pretty Berkshire countryside.

However, save yourself for the sting in the tail – the climb back up to the ridge of Walbury Hill. The run starts with a visit to the atmospheric and grisly Combe Gibbet which stands proud on an often blustery ridge with wonderful views over the surrounding countryside. It then descends gently into the valley along the Test Way, passes the 12th Century church of St Swithins and the entrance to Combe Manor (expect some startled pheasants!), winds through Combe village and finally climbs back up to the ridge and over Walbury Hill to the car park and those spectacular views.

Facilities and safety

There is a free car park at the start near Combe Gibbet. Be prepared for strong winds up on the ridge. The route can get muddy in places and there are some stony paths to negotiate, especially on the bridleway heading down to Combe Village. Trail shoes are recommended.

Interesting information

First erected in 1676, Combe Gibbet was actually only used once and the current one is a replica of the original. Married man George Broomham and widow Dorothy Newman were hanged in Winchester in 1676 and their dead bodies were then hung on either side of the gibbet to act as a grim deterrent to others. They were having an affair and the most common story is that they were brought to justice for murdering George's wife and young son when they came across them together on the Downs.

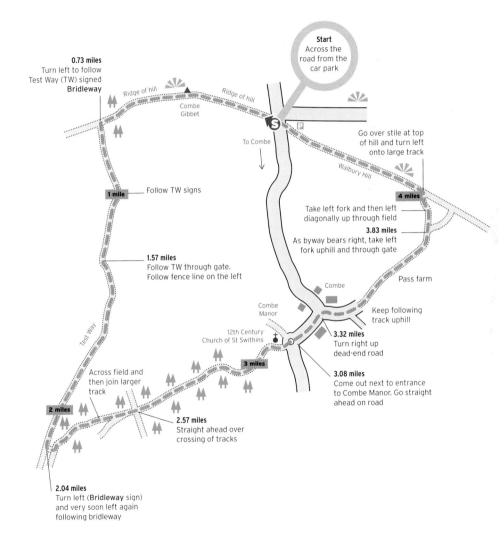

Start
Across the road from the car park

0.73 miles
Turn left to follow Test Way (TW) signed **Bridleway**

Ridge of hill

Combe Gibbet

Ridge of hill

To Combe

Go over stile at top of hill and turn left onto large track

Walbury Hill

1 mile
Follow TW signs

4 miles

Take left fork and then left diagonally up through field

3.83 miles
As byway bears right, take left fork uphill and through gate

1.57 miles
Follow TW through gate. Follow fence line on the left

Pass farm

Combe

Combe Manor

Keep following track uphill

Test Way

12th Century Church of St Swithins

3.32 miles
Turn right up dead-end road

3 miles

Across field and then join larger track

3.08 miles
Come out next to entrance to Combe Manor. Go straight ahead on road

2 miles

2.57 miles
Straight ahead over crossing of tracks

2.04 miles
Turn left (**Bridleway** sign) and very soon left again following bridleway

12 Rolling Ogbourne Downs

An undulating run over rolling downs with fantastic views

Distance: **8.37 miles/13.47 km** | Undulating | **MODERATE**

Flat equiv.: **8.91 miles/14.34 km** | Climb rate: **17m/mile**

Terrain: **Quiet road, wide tracks and trails**

Parking: **Free roadside parking along High Street, Ogbourne St George**

Post code: **SN8 1SL** | Grid Ref: **SU 203742**

Start: **Parklands Hotel, High Street, Ogbourne St George**

If you're looking for a nice, simple to follow, but fairly long run then this route could be for you. Fantastic views from Smeathe's Ridge overlooking the chalk-based Marlborough Downs are the overriding feature of this run.

The route follows the ancient Ridgeway up to and along Smeathe's Ridge and then back along the top of Ogbourne Maizey Down, next to the Racecourse Gallops, before finishing up along the flat Chiseldon and Marlborough railway path, created on the track bed of the old railway line which closed in the 1960s.

Facilities and safety

There is free roadside parking along the High Street in Ogbourne St George. Refreshments are available at Parklands Hotel or The Inn with The Well. Be aware that the Downs are exposed and so it can get very breezy. Some paths can get muddy and some are fairly stony. Trail shoes are recommended.

Interesting information

The Ridgeway is 87 miles long and much of it, including Smeathe's Ridge, was originally used as a route by prehistoric man. The original track actually stretched much further, about 250 miles from the Dorset coast to the Wash on the Norfolk coast, and its attraction was the higher ground which was less wooded and drier than other routes.

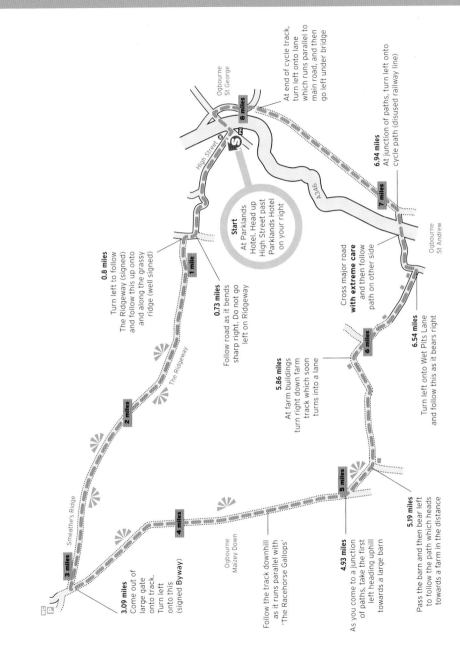

Start
At Parklands Hotel. Head up High Street past Parklands Hotel on your right

0.73 miles
Follow road as it bends sharp right. Do not go left on Ridgeway

0.8 miles
Turn left to follow The Ridgeway (signed) and follow this up onto and along the grassy ridge (well signed)

3.09 miles
Come out of large gate onto track. Turn left onto this (signed **Byway**)

4.93 miles
As you come to a junction of paths, take the first left heading uphill towards a large barn

Follow the track downhill as it runs parallel with 'The Racehorse Gallops'

5.19 miles
Pass the barn and then bear left to follow the path which heads towards a farm in the distance

6.54 miles
Turn left onto Wet Pits Lane and follow this as it bears right

Cross major road **with extreme care** and then follow path on other side

5.86 miles
At farm buildings turn right down farm track which soon turns into a lane

6.94 miles
At junction of paths, turn left onto cycle path (disused railway line)

At end of cycle track, turn left onto lane which runs parallel to main road, and then go left under bridge

Ogbourne St George

Ogbourne St Andrew

Ogbourne Maizey Down

Smeathe's Ridge

The Ridgeway

High Street

A346

1 mile
2 miles
3 miles
4 miles
5 miles
6 miles
7 miles
8 miles

13 Ebbor Gorge Lookout

A challenging run rewarded with spectacular views

Distance: **4.84 miles/7.79 km** | **Hilly** | **HARD**

Flat equiv.: **5.66 miles/9.11 km** | Climb rate: **45m/mile**

Terrain: **Trail, cross country and road**

Parking: **Free parking in Wookey Hole**

Post code: **BA5 1BY** | Grid Ref: **ST 532476**

Start: **Corner of High Street, near School Hill**

This is a route of two halves! The first half features a lot of really tough climbing through the Ebbor Woods, with some steps, but you're rewarded by the fantastic viewpoint over Ebbor Gorge.

The run continues upwards before soon levelling out and there follows a fairly easy flat recovery section to the halfway point. The return is via grassy fields with grazing livestock and the last mile features an amazing downhill section with views way across Somerset and back towards Wookey Hole. Just be careful not to twist an ankle as you run joyfully back down across the grass, and take careful note of the direction of the arrows to find the next stile or gate as there is no distinct path at this point.

Facilities and safety

There is free parking at Wookey Hole, and toilets, a picnic area and a cafe nearby. Wookey Hole is a good place to take the family, with the cave to visit, a paper mill and other attractions. A few miles away is the famous Cheddar Gorge and caves. The climb up can be stony and there are often fairly muddy patches, particularly around the gates and stiles. There are herds of cows on the return section, so take the usual precautions, especially if running with a dog. Take obvious care next to the cliff edge – it's a long way down! Trail shoes are recommended.

Interesting information

Ebbor Gorge is a dry limestone gorge designated as an SSSI, formed when a huge cavern collapsed. Unlike Cheddar Gorge it is not accessible by road so the only way to see it is on foot. There are many caves in the Mendip Hills due to the particular geology of the area and another is the Wookey Hole Caves over which you will be running. This cave system was formed through erosion of the limestone hills by the River Axe.

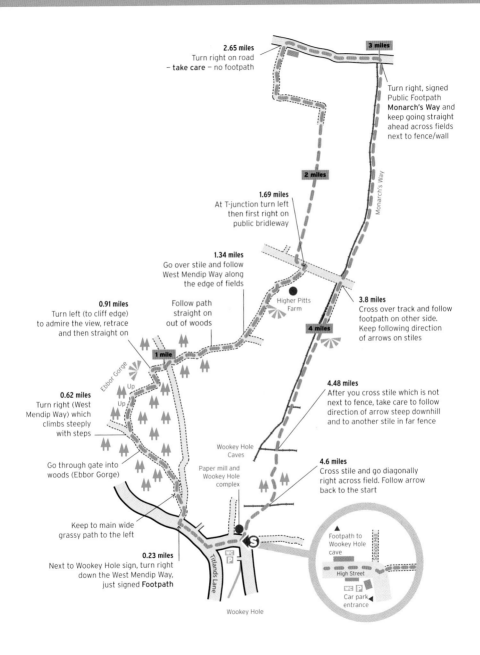

2.65 miles
Turn right on road
– **take care** – no footpath

3 miles

Turn right, signed
Public Footpath
Monarch's Way and
keep going straight
ahead across fields
next to fence/wall

Monarch's Way

2 miles

1.69 miles
At T-junction turn left
then first right on
public bridleway

1.34 miles
Go over stile and follow
West Mendip Way along
the edge of fields

Higher Pitts
Farm

3.8 miles
Cross over track and follow
footpath on other side.
Keep following direction
of arrows on stiles

0.91 miles
Turn left (to cliff edge)
to admire the view, retrace
and then straight on

Follow path
straight on
out of woods

4 miles

1 mile

Ebbor Gorge

Up

0.62 miles
Turn right (West
Mendip Way) which
climbs steeply
with steps

Up

4.48 miles
After you cross stile which is not
next to fence, take care to follow
direction of arrow steep downhill
and to another stile in far fence

Go through gate into
woods (Ebbor Gorge)

Wookey Hole
Caves

Paper mill and
Wookey Hole
complex

4.6 miles
Cross stile and go diagonally
right across field. Follow arrow
back to the start

Keep to main wide
grassy path to the left

Footpath to
Wookey Hole
cave

S

0.23 miles
Next to Wookey Hole sign, turn right
down the West Mendip Way,
just signed **Footpath**

WC P

Titlands Lane

High Street

WC P
Car park
entrance

Wookey Hole

14 Bristol's Avon Gorge

The beautiful Avon Gorge and Brunel's masterpiece

Distance: **4.57 miles/7.51 km** | Hilly | **MODERATE**

Flat equiv.: **5.09 miles/8.19 km** | Climb rate: **24m/mile**

Terrain: **Road and trail**

Parking: **Roadside parking on Promenade Road**

Post code: **BS8 3NE** | Grid Ref: **ST 565734**

Start: **Promenade opposite Percival Road**

This run is centred around the Avon Gorge which is spanned by the magnificent Clifton Suspension Bridge designed by Isambard Kingdom Brunel.

The run takes you down into the gorge and under the bridge one way, back under it the other way and, finally, after a tough but pretty climb, over it. Views of the bridge and the gorge are superb throughout.

Facilities and safety

To find the start, from Bristol follow signs to Clifton and Clifton Suspension Bridge. There is a small toll for cars that wish to cross the bridge but foot traffic is free. It used to be an annoying 2p; where would you keep it during the run? Near the start is a children's play area featuring a small stone slide (a slab of stone worn smooth by countless small, and not so small, bottoms). A larger stone slide is found on the path near the toilets and keeps children and adults amused for hours. The Observatory houses a Camera Obscura which is also worth a visit. Standard trainers are suitable for this route.

Interesting information

For the Clifton Suspension Bridge, Brunel submitted four different designs, of which the chosen Egyptian-inspired one was not actually his favourite. Many trials and tribulations followed for the builders. Work did not start until 1836 and more financial problems caused it to cease in 1853. The piers stood in splendid isolation for several years, threatened with demolition. Eventually the 700-foot bridge was completed in 1864, five years after Brunel's death.

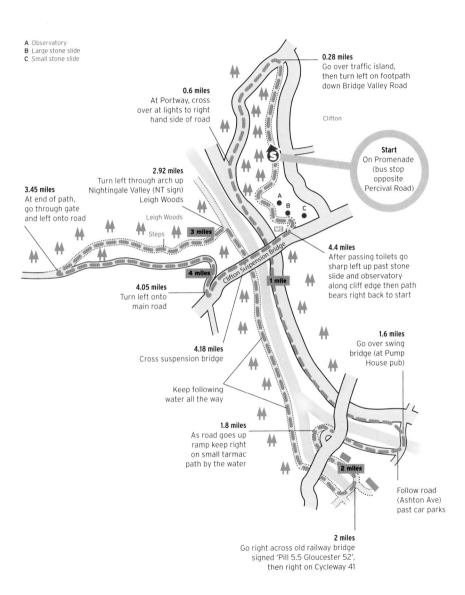

A Observatory
B Large stone slide
C Small stone slide

0.28 miles
Go over traffic island,
then turn left on footpath
down Bridge Valley Road

Clifton

0.6 miles
At Portway, cross
over at lights to right
hand side of road

Start
On Promenade
(bus stop
opposite
Percival Road)

2.92 miles
Turn left through arch up
Nightingale Valley (NT sign)
Leigh Woods

3.45 miles
At end of path,
go through gate
and left onto road

Leigh Woods

Steps

3 miles

4.4 miles
After passing toilets go
sharp left up past stone
slide and observatory
along cliff edge then path
bears right back to start

4 miles

Clifton Suspension Bridge

1 mile

4.05 miles
Turn left onto
main road

1.6 miles
Go over swing
bridge (at Pump
House pub)

4.18 miles
Cross suspension bridge

Keep following
water all the way

1.8 miles
As road goes up
ramp keep right
on small tarmac
path by the water

2 miles

Follow road
(Ashton Ave)
past car parks

2 miles
Go right across old railway bridge
signed 'Pill 5.5 Gloucester 52',
then right on Cycleway 41

15 Rhossili Bay Ramble

Superb views over 'Britain's Best Beach'

Distance: **4.00 miles/6.44 km** | Hilly | **MODERATE**

Flat equiv.: **4.60 miles/7.40 km** | Climb rate: **45m/mile**

Terrain: **Gravel and grassy trails with a short stretch of tarmac**

Parking: **Paid car park, Rhossili**

Post code: **SA3 1PP** | Grid Ref: **SS 415880**

Start: **Car park entrance**

This is a lovely run with great views over Rhossili Village, the majestic sweep of Rhossili Bay and the Worms Head Peninsula.

We quickly nip through the village before admiring the bay and water sports enthusiasts' bravery, from a good path overlooking it. The return is via a very stiff but short climb, then a ridge run across Rhossili Down with further great views, completed by a short and sharp descent back down to the village.

Facilities and safety

The start is at the entrance to a large pay on entry car park just through the village. There are toilets, a visitor centre and a shop at the south end of the car park. There are two cafes near the entrance to the car park. Standard trainers or trail shoes are suitable for this route.

Interesting information

At low tide there is a huge expanse of beach about four miles in length, and it is possible to walk across the bay to Llangennith or even cross onto the Worms Head Peninsula at low tide. There is always some sand, even at high tide. The beach is very popular with surfers and everyone else it seems, as it is constantly voted Britain's Best Beach and in the top 25 of the world's best. Nice though it is we are not convinced the likes of Ipanema, Copacabana and Bondi have too much to worry about!

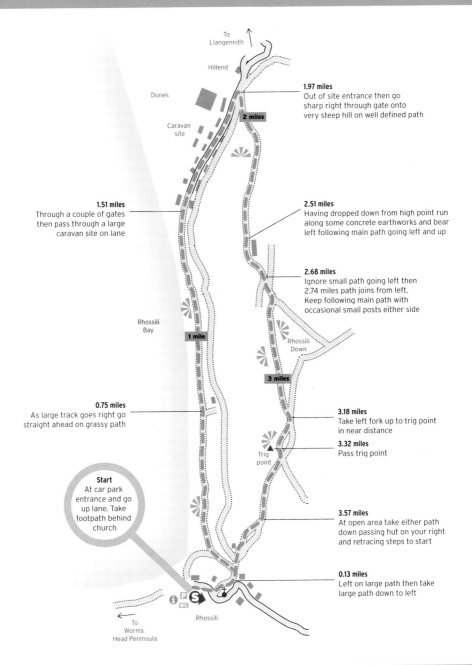

To
Llangennith

Hillend

Dunes

1.97 miles
Out of site entrance then go
sharp right through gate onto
very steep hill on well defined path

2 miles

Caravan
site

1.51 miles
Through a couple of gates
then pass through a large
caravan site on lane

2.51 miles
Having dropped down from high point run
along some concrete earthworks and bear
left following main path going left and up

2.68 miles
Ignore small path going left then
2.74 miles path joins from left.
Keep following main path with
occasional small posts either side

Rhossili
Bay

1 mile

Rhossili
Down

3 miles

0.75 miles
As large track goes right go
straight ahead on grassy path

3.18 miles
Take left fork up to trig point
in near distance

3.32 miles
Pass trig point

Trig
point

Start
At car park
entrance and go
up lane. Take
footpath behind
church

3.57 miles
At open area take either path
down passing hut on your right
and retracing steps to start

0.13 miles
Left on large path then take
large path down to left

To
Worms
Head Peninsula

Rhossili

16 Sweet Sugar Loaf

Sweeping vistas on the Brecon Beacons

Distance: **5.21 miles/8.38 km** | Hilly | **HARD**

Flat equiv.: **6.34 miles/10.20 km** | Climb rate: **58m/mile**

Terrain: **Grassy paths and some trail**

Parking: **Free car park north of Abergavenny** (signed *Sugarloaf Vineyards*)

Post code: **NP7 7LA** | Grid Ref: **SO 268167**

Start: **Rear of car park**

While unfortunately not the same Sugar Loaf where James Bond had a memorable tiff with Jaws atop a cable car in Moonraker, the summit of this particular Sugar Loaf (at 596m) makes for a great run over the open access land of the Brecon Beacons National Park.

Although there are no stiles or gates to negotiate, the climb up to the shapely summit is certainly challenging. On a clear day, spectacular views from the summit stretch north to the Black Mountains, east to the Cotswolds, west to the Brecon Beacons and south to the Bristol Channel. There are numerous paths criss-crossing the park and this is only one suggestion from a multitude of possible routes. Go and explore!

Facilities and safety

Parking is free in a small car park up a single track road off the A40 west of Abergavenny. Initially follow signs to Sugarloaf Vineyards, before a slightly tricky drive up a narrow lane with the occasional passing place and *To Car Park* sign. There is nothing at the car park except a good view. The descent from the Sugar Loaf summit is steep and there are a few rocks around to watch out for. The temperature and wind at the top will likely be lower and higher respectively than at the start, so take a jacket, whistle and compass.

Interesting information

The Sugar Loaf – *Mynydd Pen-y-Fal* in Welsh – is the most southerly summit of the Black Mountains and sits on National Trust land, the Trust managing the grazing of Welsh mountain sheep on its flanks. The upper slopes are bedecked in fern, heather and bilberry, while on the lower slopes you'll find deciduous mixed woodland. The sign at the car park lists running as one of the things you can do on open access land ... which is good to know!

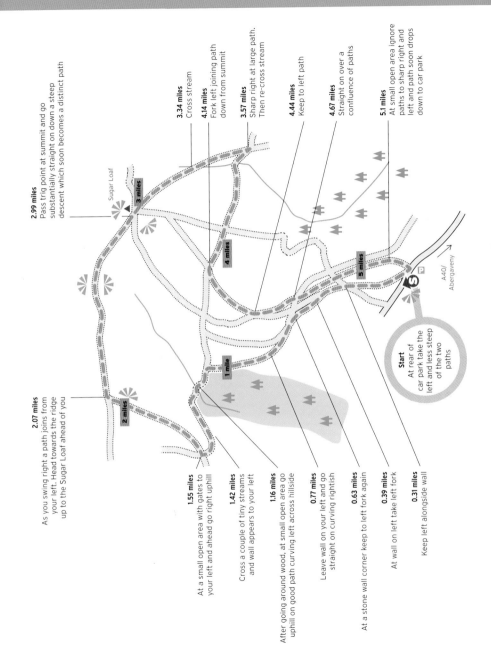

2.99 miles
Pass trig point at summit and go substantially straight on down a steep descent which soon becomes a distinct path

3.34 miles
Cross stream

4.14 miles
Fork left joining path down from summit

3.57 miles
Sharp right at large path. Then re-cross stream

4.44 miles
Keep to left path

4.67 miles
Straight on over a confluence of paths

5.1 miles
At small open area ignore paths to sharp right and left and path soon drops down to car park

Sugar Loaf

3 miles

4 miles

5 miles

A40/
Abergavenny

Start
At rear of car park take the left and less steep of the two paths

1 mile

2 miles

2.07 miles
As you swing right a path joins from your left. Head towards the ridge up to the Sugar Loaf ahead of you

1.55 miles
At a small open area with gates to your left and ahead go right uphill

1.42 miles
Cross a couple of tiny streams and wall appears to your left

1.16 miles
After going around wood, at small open area go uphill on good path curving left across hillside

0.77 miles
Leave wall on your left and go straight on curving rightish

0.63 miles
At a stone wall corner keep to left fork again

0.39 miles
At wall on left take left fork

0.31 miles
Keep left alongside wall

Northern
England
& Wales

Our routes in this section again mirror the great diversity of the British landscape. There is something for everyone, from Yorkshire's moors and industrial heritage, to Lakeland's beautiful scenery, to the magnificent coastal routes and castles of Northumberland. Many routes feature stiff climbs and others easy trails, but whichever route you choose we guarantee you an unforgettable run.

OTLEY SURPRISE

PHOTO: BEN WINSTON

1 STOODLEY PIKE STAGGER 2 MAWDDACH TRAIL MEANDER 3 ABER FALLS AMBLE 4 HOLKHAM'S ENDLESS SANDS
5 WANDER WORDSWORTH'S LAKES PHOTO: JOHN COEFIELD

6 ROBIN HOOD'S BAY 7 THE DEVIL'S HOLE PHOTO: JOHN COEFIELD 8 DUNSTANBURGH CASTLE CANTER 9 BASSENTHWAITE LAKE 10 PEN-Y-GHENT ACSENT
11 CHATSWORTH COUNTRYSIDE PHOTO: JOHN COEFIELD

17 Hambleton Peninsula

A pleasant undulating run surrounded by lovely waterside views

Distance: **4.63 miles/7.45 km** | Undulating | **MODERATE**

Flat equiv.: **4.88 miles/7.85 km** | Climb rate: **15m/mile**

Terrain: **Well maintained cycle track and road**

Parking: **Free roadside parking in Upper Hambleton**

Post code: **LE15 8TL** | Grid Ref: **SK 900075**

Start: **With church to your right, and run south (slightly downhill)**

This is a simple to follow and scenic route around the Hambleton Peninsula, overlooking Rutland Water.

Apart from just under a mile of country lanes, the rest is on a good and popular cycling track that undulates around the perimeter. There are great views throughout almost the entire route and the vastness of the reservoir of Rutland Water can be truly appreciated.

Facilities and safety

There is free parking along the lanes in Upper Hambleton, although this is a popular place for walking and cycling so it can get busy. There are sheep grazing on much of the route so dogs need to be kept on leads. Also, keep an eye out for cyclists zooming past. Standard trainers should be ok for this route.

Interesting information

Rutland Water is one of the largest man-made lakes in Europe and is located in Rutland, England's smallest county. It was built in the 1970s to supply water to the growing populations and industry in the East Midlands utilising water from the lower reaches of the rivers Nene and Welland. Hambleton originally included Upper Hambleton, Middle Hambleton and Nether Hambleton, however the latter two were almost completely submerged when the reservoir was created.

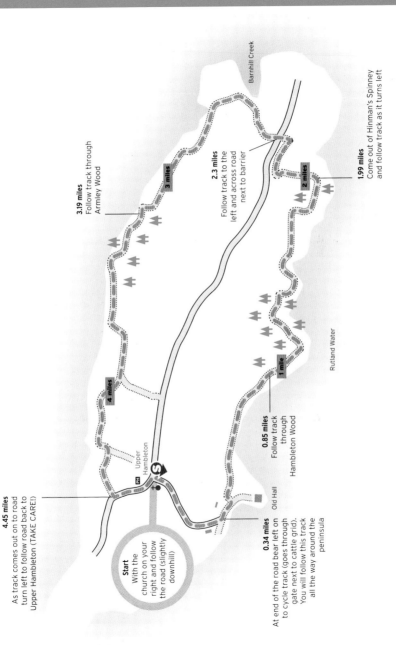

Barnhill Creek

3.19 miles
Follow track through Armley Wood

3 miles

2.3 miles
Follow track to the left and across road next to barrier

1.99 miles
Come out of Hinman's Spinney and follow track as it turns left

2 miles

4 miles

Rutland Water

1 mile

0.85 miles
Follow track through Hambleton Wood

Upper Hambleton

Old Hall

4.45 miles
As track comes out on to road turn left to follow road back to Upper Hambleton (TAKE CARE!)

Start
With the church on your right and follow the road (slightly downhill)

0.34 miles
At end of the road bear left on to cycle track (goes through gate next to cattle grid). You will follow this track all the way around the peninsula

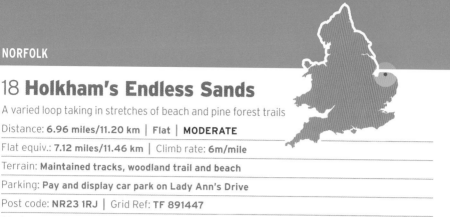

18 Holkham's Endless Sands

A varied loop taking in stretches of beach and pine forest trails

Distance: **6.96 miles/11.20 km** | **Flat** | **MODERATE**

Flat equiv.: **7.12 miles/11.46 km** | Climb rate: **6m/mile**

Terrain: **Maintained tracks, woodland trail and beach**

Parking: **Pay and display car park on Lady Ann's Drive**

Post code: **NR23 1RJ** | Grid Ref: **TF 891447**

Start: **First track on the left, after the gates**

A varied run in a loop around the seemingly endless Holkham beach and Nature Reserve. The run starts off with a mainly sheltered trot through the narrow pine forest with the opportunity for a spot of bird watching from the hides en route.

There follows a two-mile stretch along the vast Holkham beach, with spectacular views over the North Sea from the point where the Vikings landed in the first millennium. After running past and admiring the row of pretty, brightly coloured beach huts at Wells-Next-The-Sea, the return tracks along the edge of the pine forest.

Facilities and safety

There is a large pay and display car park along Lady Ann's Drive and a refreshment hut at peak times. The run consists of wide, signed tracks, narrow winding trails through the pine trees and beach running. Some parts of the beach consist of soft sand and sand dunes, but this is fairly easy to avoid if you wish. Not surprisingly, the wind can be fairly strong off the North Sea.

Interesting information

Holkham Nature Reserve comprises a number of rare and precious habitats, including salt marsh, sand dunes, pine woodland, beach and grazing marsh. The present landscape was reclaimed in the late 19th century by the 2nd Earl of Leicester. To achieve this he planted three miles of sand with Corsican pine trees to stabilise the dunes and hold back the sea. The original sea wall was further inland.

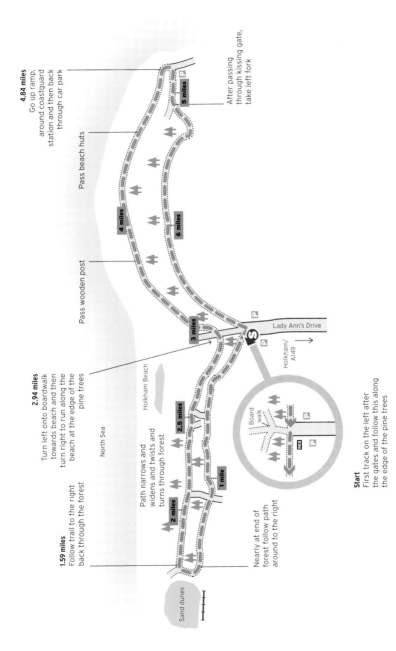

4.84 miles
Go up ramp, around coastguard station and then back through car park

After passing through kissing gate, take left fork

Pass beach huts

5 miles

4 miles

6 miles

Pass wooden post

3 miles

Lady Ann's Drive

Holkham/ A149

2.94 miles
Turn left onto boardwalk towards beach and then turn right to run along the beach at the edge of the pine trees

Holkham Beach

North Sea

Board walk

2.5 miles

1.59 miles
Follow trail to the right back through the forest

Path narrows and widens and twists and turns through forest

1 mile

2 miles

Nearly at end of forest follow path around to the right

Start
First track on the left after the gates and follow this along the edge of the pine trees

Sand dunes

19 Mawddach Trail Meander

Pancake flat run with great estuary views

Distance: **6.62 miles/10.65 km** | **Flat** | EASY

Flat equiv.: **6.62 miles/10.65 km** | Climb rate: **0m/mile**

Terrain: **Good gravel trails**

Parking: **Free car park, Penmaenpool**

Post code: **LL40 1YD** | Grid Ref: **SH 694184**

Start: **By George III Hotel, Penmaenpool**

I think we can say without rebuttal that many routes along dismantled railway tracks can be a little dull and uninspiring.

Well this one is different; this flat run along a footpath, which doubles as a Sustrans cycle track, has views across the most beautiful estuary. Furthermore, the run is bookended by, at one end, the picturesque Barmouth Bridge and at the other by a Grade II listed wooden toll bridge at Penmaenpool.

Facilities and safety

Parking is available near the George III Hotel and there is an information centre in the car park. The wooden decked bridge across the estuary has a toll for cars and pedestrians (currently 60p and 20p respectively), although at the time of writing it's up for sale along with the keeper's cottage. This run can be started from the George III Hotel in Penmaenpool, running west to Barmouth, or vice versa as a point-to-point run. Alternatively you can run a variety of distances out and back from the George. Barmouth Bridge has a small toll for pedestrians at the Barmouth end.

Interesting information

Barmouth Bridge is 820m in length and originally opened in 1867. In 1980 heavy locomotive-hauled trains were banned from crossing the ageing wooden bridge thanks to damage caused by shipworms – *Teredo navalis* – boring holes in the timbers of the bridge to secrete their larvae. This is the same species of worm said to have inspired Marc Isambard Brunel to design revolutionary tunnelling shield technology used to create the Thames Tunnel, completed in 1843. Marc, the father of Isambard Kingdom Brunel, had observed the worms and their underwater tunnelling antics while working at a shipyard.

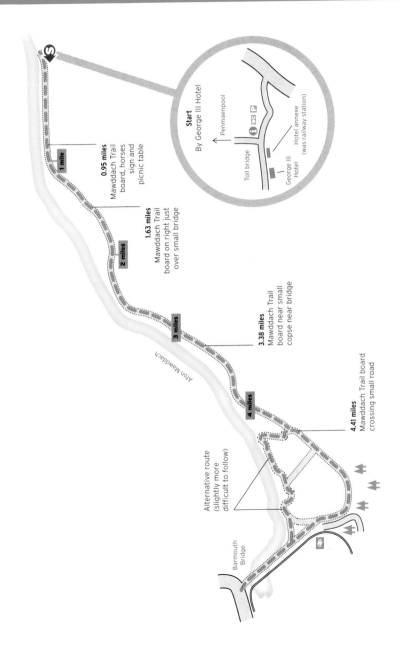

S

1 mile

0.95 miles
Mawddach Trail
board, horses
sign and
picnic table

1.63 miles
Mawddach Trail
board on right just
over small bridge

2 miles

3.38 miles
Mawddach Trail
board near small
copse near bridge

3 miles

Afon Mawddach

4 miles

4.41 miles
Mawddach Trail board
crossing small road

Alternative route
(slightly more
difficult to follow)

Barmouth
Bridge

Start
By George III Hotel

Pennmaenpool

Toll bridge

George III
Hotel

Hotel annexe
(was railway station)

20 Aber Falls Amble

Not just the spectacular Aber Falls ...

Distance: **4.11 miles/6.61 km** | Hilly | **HARD**

Flat equiv.: **4.84 miles/7.79 km** | Climb rate: **48m/mile**

Terrain: **Gravel paths, cross country and short quiet lane**

Parking: **Pay and display car park at start, on the minor road from Abergwyngregyn**

Post code: **LL33 0LP** | Grid Ref: **SH 663719**

Start: **On obvious gravel path towards Aber Falls alongside stream**

This is a lovely run visiting the splendid Aber Falls (Rhaeadr Fawr in Welsh) as well as exploring the pretty valley and taking in expansive views over to the coast.

The tracks are mainly good but there are a few rocky and slightly muddy stretches and a section on a quiet lane. The clockwise route direction we have chosen features an extended but steady climb with a short precipitous descent, with Aber Falls reached early on. If run anti-clockwise the climb is shorter but much steeper before gently descending to pass the falls with only a mile to go.

Facilities and safety

There is pay and display parking at the start and further car parking 100m up the road. Toilets and picnic tables are available near the start, and there's also a cafe in the tourist information centre at Abergwyngregyn village a short distance back down the lane.

Interesting information

The Afon Goch falls over an escarpment 120 feet high into a marshy area where two tributaries merge. The enlarged stream, Afon Rhaeadr Fawr, then heads towards the Menai Strait, part way down becoming known as the Afon Aber. In winter the falls can freeze solid enough to attract ice climbers. Many lovely pictures of the area and falls are on display in the cafe including a vintage shot of intrepid ice climbers halfway up.

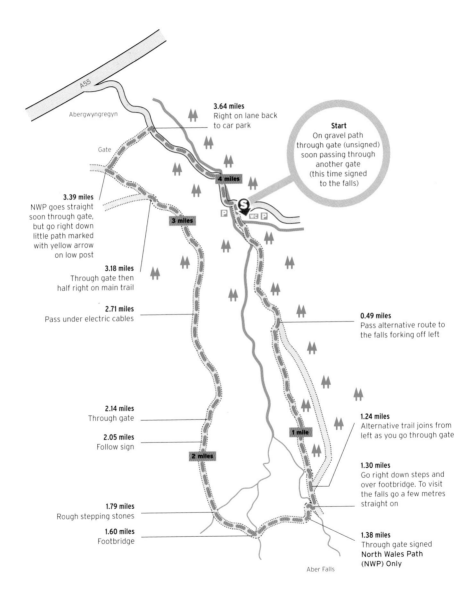

A55

Abergwyngregyn

3.64 miles
Right on lane back
to car park

Gate

Start
On gravel path
through gate (unsigned)
soon passing through
another gate
(this time signed
to the falls)

3.39 miles
NWP goes straight
soon through gate,
but go right down
little path marked
with yellow arrow
on low post

4 miles

P   wc   P

3 miles

3.18 miles
Through gate then
half right on main trail

2.71 miles
Pass under electric cables

0.49 miles
Pass alternative route to
the falls forking off left

2.14 miles
Through gate

2.05 miles
Follow sign

2 miles

1 mile

1.24 miles
Alternative trail joins from
left as you go through gate

1.30 miles
Go right down steps and
over footbridge. To visit
the falls go a few metres
straight on

1.79 miles
Rough stepping stones

1.60 miles
Footbridge

1.38 miles
Through gate signed
North Wales Path
(NWP) Only

Aber Falls

ABER FALLS AMBLE

21 Clumber Lake Loop

A lovely flat lakeside run

Distance: **3.67 miles/5.90 km** | **Flat** | EASY

Flat equiv.: **3.76 miles/6.05 km** | Climb rate: **7m/mile**

Terrain: **Trail with a short stretch of lane**

Parking: **Various options, see below**

Post code: **S80 3AZ** | Grid Ref: **SK 638753**

Start: **On lakeside path behind toilets**

Clumber Park is situated at the northernmost part of Sherwood Forest and is renowned for its magnificent display of colours during the autumn.

The 3,800 acres of the National Trust's Park include the three mile long Limetree Avenue, which is especially gorgeous in autumn, many woodland trails, and the trail around the lake of course. The lap of Clumber Park Lake is mostly on good gravel paths with a short section of tarmac. The park is very popular and can get quite crowded with all manner of folk walking, cycling and generally enjoying themselves.

Facilities and safety

The parking at the start in Hardwick Village or in the other car parks around the lake entails passing a National Trust 'checkpoint' that will charge a hefty fee unless you are an NT member. Parking further away from the lake is free, including along the stunning Limetree Avenue. Pedestrian entry is also free. There are toilets at the start and at the large car park near the chapel where there is also a visitor centre, restaurant, cafe, exhibition and bike hire.

Interesting information

Sadly Clumber House itself was demolished in 1938, a decision taken by the Earl of Lincoln who had inherited it. The local paper reported that 'the decision to completely demolish the mansion has been taken with great reluctance by the present owner ... but it has been necessitated by heavy taxation'.

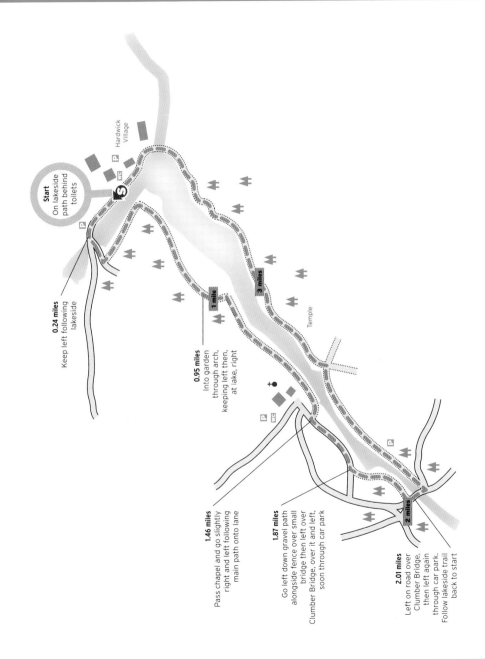

Start
On lakeside
path behind
toilets

Hardwick
Village

0.24 miles
Keep left following
lakeside

0.95 miles
Into garden
through arch,
keeping left then,
at lake, right

1 mile

3 miles

Temple

1.46 miles
Pass chapel and go slightly
right and left following
main path onto lane

1.87 miles
Go left down gravel path
alongside fence over small
bridge then left over
Clumber Bridge, over it and left,
soon through car park

2 miles

2.01 miles
Left on road over
Clumber Bridge,
then left again
through car park.
Follow lakeside trail
back to start

22 Cromford Four

Industrial heritage in a nutshell

Distance: **4 miles/6.44 km** | Hilly | **HARD**

Flat equiv.: **4.57 miles/7.35 km** | Climb rate: **39m/mile**

Terrain: **Towpath, trail and road**

Parking: **Various options, see below**

Post code: **DE4 3RP** | Grid Ref: **SK 300570**

Start: **Cromford Wharf**

This run starts off flat as the proverbial pancake along the canal, before turning and joining the High Peak Trail for a lung-busting mile-long climb.

The top rewards the runner with great views, followed by a bit of respite on the flat. A hell-for-leather road descent into Cromford completes the circuit.

Facilities and safety

There is pay and display parking at Arkwright's Wharf, or free parking on Mill Road. There are toilets at the car park and refreshments again at Arkwright's Wharf adjacent to the start, as well as a picnic area by the canal. This route is traffic free for the first three miles, but care must be taken crossing very minor roads on the descent, as well as the A6 at the bottom; please use the pedestrian crossing and take care. Standard trainers are suitable for this route.

Interesting information

Sir Richard Arkwright is often credited as being the father of the industrial revolution. In 1771 he and his partners built the world's first water-powered cotton mill at Cromford. The Cromford Canal was opened in 1794 supported by Arkwright as he needed easier access to Liverpool for bringing in raw cotton; a quicker way of sending his thread to the knitters of Nottingham and the opening up of more markets. He lived at Rock House in Cromford, opposite his original mill.

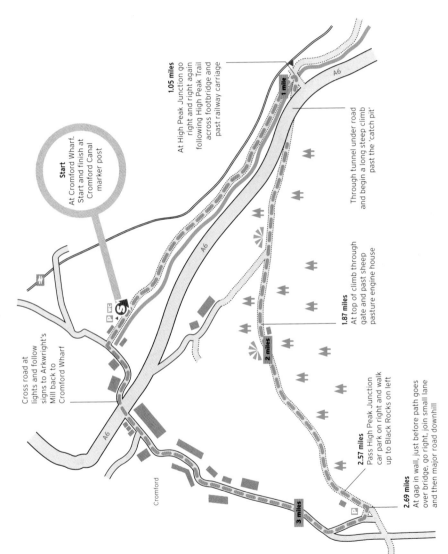

Start
At Cromford Wharf.
Start and finish at
Cromford Canal
marker post

1.05 miles
At High Peak Junction go
right and right again
following High Peak Trail
across footbridge and
past railway carriage

Through tunnel under road
and begin a long steep climb
past the 'catch pit'

1 mile

A6

1.87 miles
At top of climb through
gate and past sheep
pasture engine house

2 miles

Cross road at
lights and follow
signs to Arkwright's
Mill back to
Cromford Wharf

A6

2.57 miles
Pass High Peak Junction
car park on right and walk
up to Black Rocks on left

2.69 miles
At gap in wall, just before path goes
over bridge, go right, join small lane
and then major road downhill

Cromford

3 miles

23 **Chatsworth Countryside**

A glorious jaunt overlooking Chatsworth House

Distance: **6.39 miles/10.28 km** | Hilly | **MODERATE**

Flat equiv.: **6.9 miles/11.01 km** | Climb rate: **21m/mile**

Terrain: **Parkland, cross country, trail and a short section of road**

Parking: **Car park, Baslow**

Post code: **DE45 1SR** | Grid Ref: **SK 258721**

Start: **Car park, Baslow**

Wonderful views over the stunning Chatsworth House, home to the Duke and Duchess of Devonshire, and the surrounding parkland are the most memorable features of this run.

This route takes you through the open parkland, alongside the River Derwent, up and over nearby farmland with views back down to the House and then returns via the attractive and interesting village of Edensor.

Facilities and safety

There is pay and display parking and toilets in Baslow. Entry to the grounds of the House is free using the footpaths shown. There are shops and cafes in Baslow, and a nice cafe at Chatsworth House. Dogs should be kept on leads in the park. Trail shoes are recommended as some paths can get a little muddy at times.

Interesting information

Edensor was originally located closer to Chatsworth House but was relocated to its present position as it 'spoilt' the view from the house. Most of the buildings date from around 1840 and were re-built at the command of the 6th Duke of Devonshire. Apparently every house was built to a different design, certainy worth checking out! Today Chatsworth is still home to the latest Duke and Duchess of Devonshire, and has been passed down through 16 generations of the Cavendish family. The house architecture and collection have been evolving for five centuries.

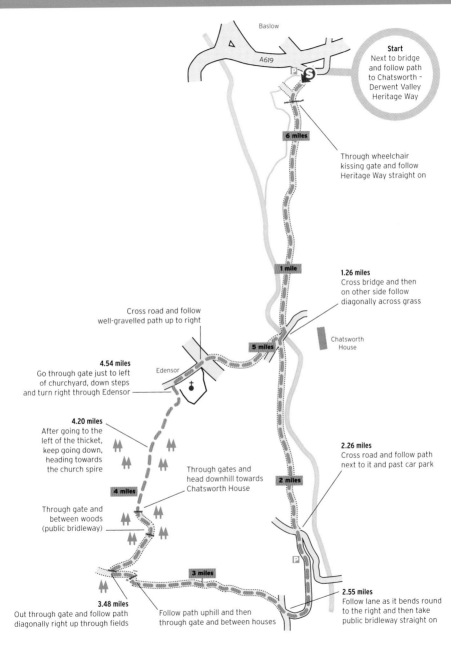

Baslow

A619

Start
Next to bridge
and follow path
to Chatsworth –
Derwent Valley
Heritage Way

6 miles

Through wheelchair
kissing gate and follow
Heritage Way straight on

1 mile

1.26 miles
Cross bridge and then
on other side follow
diagonally across grass

Chatsworth
House

Cross road and follow
well-gravelled path up to right

5 miles

Edensor

4.54 miles
Go through gate just to left
of churchyard, down steps
and turn right through Edensor

4.20 miles
After going to the
left of the thicket,
keep going down,
heading towards
the church spire

2.26 miles
Cross road and follow path
next to it and past car park

Through gates and
head downhill towards
Chatsworth House

2 miles

4 miles

Through gate and
between woods
(public bridleway)

2.55 miles
Follow lane as it bends round
to the right and then take
public bridleway straight on

3 miles

3.48 miles
Out through gate and follow path
diagonally right up through fields

Follow path uphill and then
through gate and between houses

24 **Darcy Dash**

Varied running around Lyme Park Estate and beyond

Distance: **4.10 miles/6.6 km** | Hilly | **MODERATE**

Flat equiv.: **4.67 miles/7.51 km** | Climb rate: **37m/mile**

Terrain: **Trail, lane and cross country**

Parking: **Car park, Lyme Park**

Post code: **SK12 2NR** (see note below*) | Grid Ref: **SJ 962824**

Start: **Junction of lanes by car park, Lyme Park**

This is a tough but rewarding route centred on the National Trust's Lyme Park in Cheshire.

The run features climbs across the estate, through woodland and over moorland before plummeting down a very quiet lane. Then, having crossed farmland, it returns back into the estate for a visit to 'The Cage' and Darcy's House.

Facilities and safety

* Note that using the postcode for SatNav can be misleading; the only vehicular entrance is off the A6 Buxton Road West, near Disley. Parking for non National Trust members is quite expensive, but entry for pedestrians is free, so you could park and start in Disley and make it a longer run down the A6 and in the gate towards the house. There is also free entry to the park in winter when the house is closed. There are refreshments, a shop and toilets near the lake. Standard trainers are suitable for this route.

Interesting information

Lyme Hall was used to represent Pemberley, the seat of Mr Darcy, in the 1995 BBC adaptation of Jane Austen's novel Pride and Prejudice. A walk to the far side of the South Lake reveals a memorable view of the hall reflected in the waters, used in the production. Perhaps more surprisingly, the Hall was also used as a location for the Red Dwarf episode 'Timeslides', as well as numerous other productions.

Lyme Hall was originally a remote hunting lodge. In Tudor times a house was built there and this was turned into an Italianate palace by the Venetian architect Leoni in the early 18th Century.

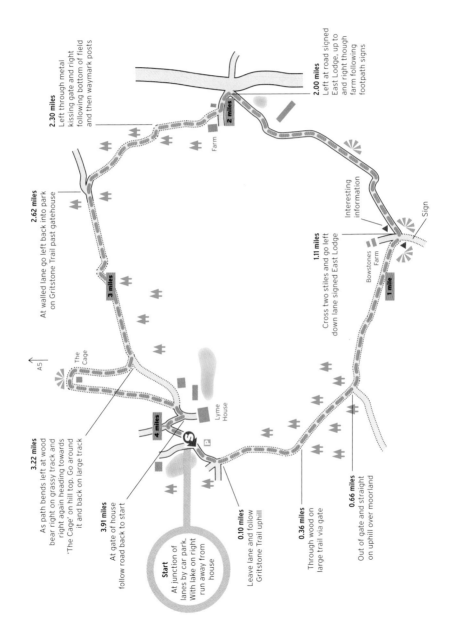

2.30 miles
Left through metal kissing gate and right following bottom of field and then waymark posts

2.00 miles
Left at road signed East Lodge, up to and right through farm following footpath signs

2.62 miles
At walled lane go left back into park on Gritstone Trail past gatehouse

Farm

2 miles

Interesting information

1.11 miles
Cross two stiles and go left down lane signed East Lodge

Sign

Bowstones Farm

1 mile

3.22 miles
As path bends left at wood bear right on grassy track and right again heading towards 'The Cage' on hill top. Go around it and back on large track

The Cage

A5

3 miles

3.91 miles
At gate of house follow road back to start

Lyme House

4 miles

Start
At junction of lanes by car park. With lake on right run away from house

0.10 miles
Leave lane and follow Gritstone Trail uphill

0.36 miles
Through wood on large trail via gate

0.66 miles
Out of gate and straight on uphill over moorland

25 **Rivington Pike**

Climb to the tower for great Pennine views

Distance: **5.26 miles/8.46 km** | Hilly | **HARD**

Flat equiv.: **5.98 miles/9.62 km** | Climb rate: **36m/mile**

Terrain: **Mostly trail with short stretches of cross country and lane**

Parking: **Free parking, Great House Barn**

Post code: **BL6 7RZ** | Grid Ref: **SD 628139**

Start: **On small lane, opposite The Great House Barn Cafe**

As you might expect, this run up to Rivington Pike on the West Pennine Moors has plenty of climbing, but the good news is that most of it takes place in the first third of the run.

There is a lovely downhill to look forward to and a nice flat return alongside the banks of Rivington reservoir. As it is quite exposed up at the top of the Pike it would be best to tackle this route on a clear day if possible and we advise taking and wearing sensible equipment, and also avoid running alone. The views when you make it, however, are spectacular.

Facilities and safety

There is free parking at Great House Barn and nearby where there is also a cafe and toilets. Many of the large tracks are stony and a little difficult to run along and, as with many off-road routes, be prepared for a little mud.

Interesting information

Built in 1733 the Grade II listed Rivington Pike Tower was formerly used as a hunting lodge by Squire John Andrews, sheltering shooting parties out on a jolly from Rivington Hall. Rivington Castle is actually a replica castle which was built on the orders of Lord Leverhulme, who founded the Lever Brothers soap and cleaning product firm. A somewhat authoritarian figure he controlled his workers lives in the model village of Port Sunlight on Merseyside saying, *'a good workman may have a wife of objectionable habits, or may have objectionable habits himself, which make it undesirable for us to have him in the village'.*

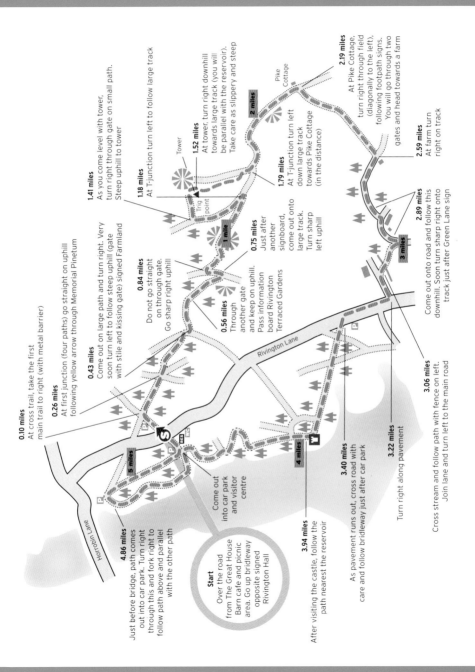

0.10 miles
At cross trail, take the first main trail to right (with metal barrier)

0.26 miles
At first junction (four paths) go straight on uphill following yellow arrow through Memorial Pinetum

0.43 miles
Come out on large path and turn right. Very soon turn left to follow steep uphill (gate with stile and kissing gate) signed Farmland

0.84 miles
Do not go straight on through gate. Go sharp right uphill

0.56 miles
Through another gate and keep on uphill. Pass information board Rivington Terraced Gardens

0.75 miles
Just after another signboard, come out onto large track. Turn sharp left uphill

1.41 miles
As you come level with tower, turn right through gate on small path. Steep uphill to tower

1.18 miles
At T-junction turn left to follow large track

Tower

Trig point

1.52 miles
At tower, turn right downhill towards large track (you will be parallel with the reservoir). Take care as slippery and steep

1.79 miles
At T-junction turn left down large track towards Pike Cottage (in the distance)

Pike Cottage

2 miles

2.19 miles
At Pike Cottage, turn right through field (diagonally to the left), following footpath signs. You will go through two gates and head towards a farm

2.59 miles
At farm turn right on track

2.89 miles

3 miles

3.06 miles
Come out onto road and follow this downhill. Soon turn sharp right onto track just after Green Lane sign

Rivington Lane

4 miles

3.22 miles
As pavement runs out, cross road with care and follow bridleway just after car park

3.40 miles
Turn right along pavement

3.94 miles
After visiting the castle, follow the path nearest the reservoir

Come out into car park and visitor centre

Start
Over the road from The Great House Barn cafe and picnic area. Go up bridleway opposite signed Rivington Hall

5 miles

Horrobin Lane

4.86 miles
Just before bridge, path comes out into car park. Turn right through this and fork right to follow path above and parallel with the other path

STOODLEY PIKE STAGGER

26 Stoodley Pike Stagger

Run to one of the Pennine Way's iconic landmarks

Distance: **5.58 miles/8.98 km** | Hilly | **EXTREME**

Flat equiv.: **6.66 miles/10.72 km** | Climb rate: **53m/mile**

Terrain: **Lane, trails and fell paths**

Parking: **Large lay-by on A646 near Todmorden**

Post code: **OL14 6DA** | Grid Ref: **SD 960248**

Start: **Shaw Wood Road**

Make no mistake, this is a challenging run up to the imposing Stoodley Pike monument.
The route starts from Todmorden and features a section of canal, quiet lanes, trails and fell paths. The climb is well worth it for the sense of achievement and of course the views.

Facilities and safety

Parking is available at a large lay-by off the A646 Halifax Road near Todmorden. If it's full, there's also the Rodwell End car park slightly closer to Todmorden. There are no amenities at the start but you are close to the village of Todmorden and not far from lively Hebden Bridge.

Interesting information

Stoodley Pike sits on a hill in the South Pennines just 400m above sea level and it is the striking monument that serves to make it a magnet for hikers, fell-runners and cyclists as well as the fact that the Pennine Way (Britain's first National Trail, opened in 1965) and Pennine Bridleway pass over it. The existing 121-foot-high monument on Stoodley Pike is actually the second to be erected as the first one fell to the ground in 1854, forty years after it was built to commemorate the defeat of Napoleon's armies at the Battle of Leipzig.

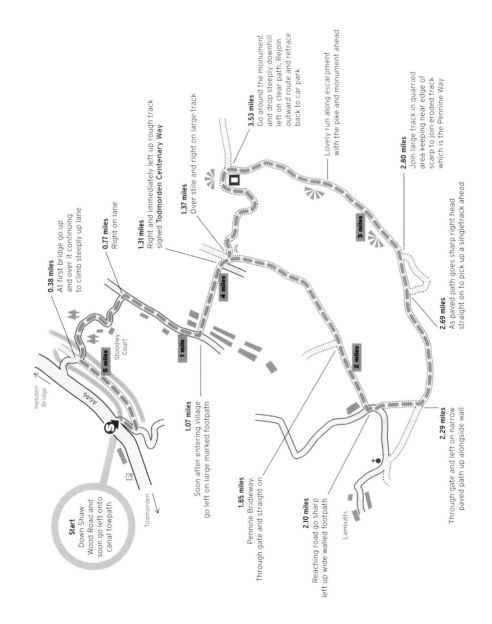

0.38 miles
At first bridge go up and over it continuing to climb steeply up lane

0.77 miles
Right on lane

1.31 miles
Right and immediately left up rough track signed **Todmorden Centenary Way**

1.37 miles
Over stile and right on large track

3.53 miles
Go around the monument and drop steeply downhill left on clear path. Rejoin outward route and retrace back to car park

Lovely run along escarpment with the pike and monument ahead

2.80 miles
Join large track in quarried area keeping near edge of scarp to join eroded track which is the Pennine Way

2.69 miles
As paved path goes sharp right head straight on to pick up a singletrack ahead

2.29 miles
Through gate and left on narrow paved path up alongside wall

2.10 miles
Reaching road go sharp left up wide walled footpath

Lambutts

1.85 miles
Pennine Bridleway. Through gate and straight on

1.07 miles
Soon after entering village go left on large marked footpath

Stoodley Court

Hebden Bridge

A646

Todmorden

Start
Down Shaw Wood Road and soon go left onto canal towpath

5 miles

1 mile

2 miles

3 miles

4 miles

27 **Otley Surprise**

Exploring the views and forest of the Chevin hillside

Distance: **3.37 miles/5.42 km** | Hilly | **HARD**

Flat equiv.: **4.08 miles/6.56 km** | Climb rate: **56m/mile**

Terrain: **Gravel trail, cross country and lane**

Parking: **Chevin Quarry car park**

Post code: **LS21 3DE** | Grid Ref: **SE 212444**

Start: **Chevin Quarry car park**

This a fairly short run, but nevertheless quite challenging as it runs up and down the full height of the Chevin, the wooded hillside overlooking the West Yorkshire town of Otley.

From the car park we follow a trail with views to the right over Otley then a short sharp ascent to Surprise View with, unsurprisingly, fantastic views over not just Otley, but the valley of Wharfedale, Barden Fell, Simon's and Lord's Seats, Norwood Top, Almscliff Crag and even York Minster. The remainder of the route features a hair-raising descent, an easy road section and a lung-busting, paved and stepped ascent.

Facilities and safety

The car parking is free at the start but there are no other amenities. See the map for other parking areas, including the large car park at Surprise View. All the car parks in the Chevin Forest Park are free. Shoes with a good grip are recommended for this route.

Interesting information

British Romantic landscape painter J. M. W. Turner (1775–1851) was inspired by a thunderstorm above Otley Chevin which he sketched on the back of an envelope. That sketch would later become one of his most famous paintings (and he painted a lot!) called, bizarrely, 'Hannibal Crossing the Alps'.

The Chevin is a favoured training area for Britain's World Championship winning and Olympic Gold and Bronze Medal winning triathletes, Alistair and Jonathan Brownlee, who live just down the road. So, although you may not be able to run like an Olympian, you can at least run in their footsteps.

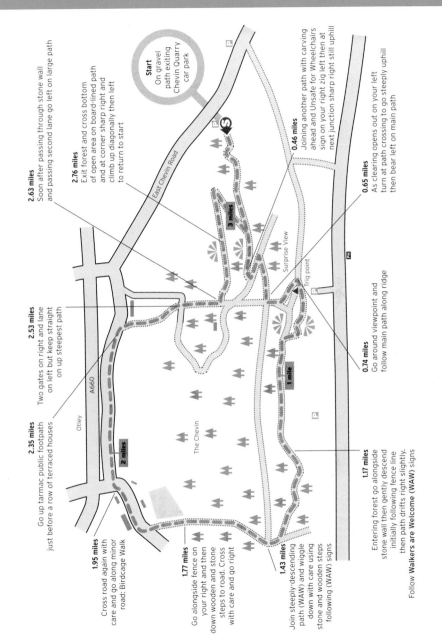

Start
On gravel
path exiting
Chevin Quarry
car park

2.63 miles
Soon after passing through stone wall
and passing second lane go left on large path

2.76 miles
Exit forest and cross bottom
of open area on board-lined path
and at corner sharp right and
climb up diagonally then left
to return to start

0.46 miles
Joining another path with carving
ahead and Unsafe for Wheelchairs
sign on your right zig left then at
next junction sharp right still uphill

0.65 miles
As clearing opens out on your left
turn at path crossing to go steeply uphill
then bear left on main path

East Chevin Road

3 miles

Surprise View

Trig point

0.74 miles
Go around viewpoint and
follow main path along ridge

2.53 miles
Two gates on right and lane
on left but keep straight
on up steepest path

A660

Otley

2 miles

1 mile

The Chevin

2.35 miles
Go up tarmac public footpath
just before a row of terraced houses

1.95 miles
Cross road again with
care and go along minor
road: Birdcage Walk

1.77 miles
Go alongside fence on
your right and then
down wooden and stone
steps to road. Cross
with care and go right

1.43 miles
Join steeply-descending
path (WAW) and wiggle
down with care using
stone and wooden steps
following (WAW) signs

1.17 miles
Entering forest go alongside
stone wall then gently descend
initially following fence line
then path drifts right slightly.
Follow **Walkers are Welcome (WAW)** signs

OTLEY SURPRISE

28 Leeds & Liverpool Canal Loop

The Pennine Way and an unusual canal

Distance: **5.71 miles/9.19 km**	**Undulating**	EASY
Flat equiv.: **5.94 miles/9.56 km**	Climb rate: **10m/mile**
Terrain: **Cross country and towpath**
Parking: **Free car park, Gargrave**
Post code: **BD23 3RJ**	Grid Ref: **SD 931543**
Start: **Next to bridge 170**

The Leeds and Liverpool Canal meanders into Gargrave following the contours of the land and thus, unusually for a canal, provides nice views across the surrounding picturesque countryside.

To get to the canal we use part of the original long distance footpath – the Pennine Way – across fields, stiles and bridges. Finally, running into the village we drop down next to the Bank Newton group of six locks.

Facilities and safety

There is a free car park at the junction of North Street and West Street in Gargrave. In the village you'll find plenty of shops and pubs, and a railway station. This section of the Pennine Way is not too tough although as it crosses fields and is popular with walkers it can get very muddy. There are also quite a few stiles to negotiate.

Interesting information

The Leeds and Liverpool canal is the longest canal in Northern England at 127 miles, with 91 locks and a summit level of 487 feet. The engineering of the canal is different from other Trans-Pennine canals, with most of the locks concentrated in groups with long, level sections between. Tunnels and cuttings are generally avoided, the canal following contours, hence the winding nature of this section. In some sections the distance between points by canal is twice the shortest distance.

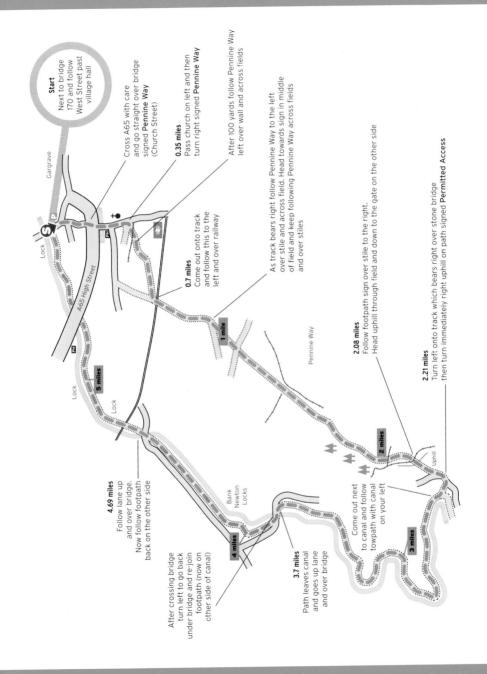

Start
Next to bridge
170 and follow
West Street past
village hall

Gargrave

Cross A65 with care
and go straight over bridge
signed **Pennine Way**
(Church Street)

0.35 miles
Pass church on left and then
turn right signed **Pennine Way**

After 100 yards follow Pennine Way
left over wall and across fields

Lock

A65 High Street

0.7 miles
Come out onto track
and follow this to the
left and over railway

As track bears right follow Pennine Way
over stile and across field. Head towards sign in middle
of field and keep following Pennine Way across fields
and over stiles

Pennine Way

1 mile

2.08 miles
Follow footpath sign over stile to the right.
Head uphill through field and down to the gate on the other side

2.21 miles
Turn left onto track which bears right over stone bridge
then turn immediately right uphill on path signed **Permitted Access**

Lock

5 miles

Lock

2 miles

Uphill

4.69 miles
Follow lane up
and over bridge.
Now follow footpath
back on the other side

Bank
Newton
Locks

After crossing bridge
turn left to go back
under bridge and re-join
footpath (now on
other side of canal)

4 miles

3.7 miles
Path leaves canal
and goes up lane
and over bridge

Come out next
to canal and follow
canal towpath with canal
on your left

3 miles

29 Pen-y-ghent ascent

A beautiful run over a Yorkshire icon

Distance: **5.92 miles/9.52 km** | Extreme | **EXTREME**

Flat equiv.: **7.58 miles/12.20 km** | Climb rate: **75m/mile**

Terrain: **Trail paths over the fell with short stretch of road**

Parking: **Pay and display, Horton in Ribblesdale**

Post code: **BD24 0HB** | Grid Ref: **SD 807725**

Start: **South on the B6479**

This is a classic route to the top of one of Yorkshire's famous three peaks (the other two being Ingleborough and Whernside).

There is good running most of the way, aside from a short scramble up to the summit and precipitous early descent. Tremendous views over the Yorkshire Dales and surrounding peaks are the reward for the undeniably stiff climb, this run being probably the toughest in this book.

Facilities and safety

The start is at a pay and display car park in the centre of Horton in Ribblesdale. A couple of pubs are situated at either end of village as well as the walker's centre, and the Pen-y-ghent cafe is on the main road. Although a relatively short run this is still an exposed fell and a bum bag with some basics is recommended; food, waterproofs, compass and whistle.

Interesting information

Completing all three peaks in under 12 hours is a popular walker's challenge, with people frequently starting this walk from Horton in Ribblesdale's Pen-y-ghent cafe. By contrast the record for the Three Peaks Fell Race is a sprightly 2 hours 29 minutes for the 24-mile route.

The distinctive shape of the peak and the ridges on its sides is due to the different types of rock strata; millstone grit on top, softer shale beneath and a band of limestone halfway up.

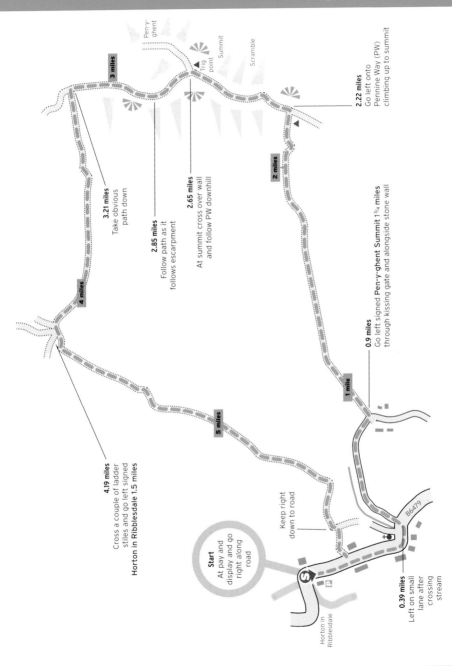

Pen-y-ghent

Summit

Scramble

Trig point

3 miles

2.22 miles
Go left onto
Pennine Way (PW)
climbing up to summit

3.21 miles
Take obvious
path down

2.85 miles
Follow path as it
follows escarpment

2.65 miles
At summit cross over wall
and follow PW downhill

2 miles

4 miles

0.9 miles
Go left signed **Pen-y-ghent Summit** 1¾ miles
through kissing gate and alongside stone wall

1 mile

5 miles

B6479

4.19 miles
Cross a couple of ladder
stiles and go left signed
Horton in Ribblesdale 1.5 miles

Keep right
down to road

Start
At pay and
display and go
right along
road

0.39 miles
Left on small
lane after
crossing
stream

Horton in
Ribblesdale

30 **Scar House Reservoir**

Easy running among spectacular scenery

Distance: **4.30 miles/6.92 km** | **Undulating** | EASY

Flat equiv.: **4.55 miles/7.32 km** | Climb rate: **15m/mile**

Terrain: **Trail and road**

Parking: **Scar House Reservoir car park (free)**

Post code: **HG3 5SW** | Grid Ref: **SE 069766**

Start: **Towards dam from car park**

Although situated among high peaks and spectacular scenery, this is a relatively easy and simple to follow circuit of Scar House reservoir in Upper Nidderdale, North Yorkshire.

You'll encounter rough and undulating stony paths along the north side with gates and stiles to negotiate, but this is balanced by a lovely fast return on a tarmac track.

Facilities and safety

Parking is at a large car park near the dam wall of Scar House Reservoir which is accessed by a lane from Lofthouse (not Middlesmoor). Keep a sharp look out for signs as you pass through and then enjoy the nice drive along the Nidd Valley to the dam. You'll find toilets at the car park and a very interesting information board. The nearest food and drink can be found at touristy Pateley Bridge (also home to the oldest sweet shop in England). Trainers with a good grip are recommended for this route.

Interesting information

Scar House Reservoir was built by Bradford Corporation to supply water to the Bradford area. Water is transferred via the Nidd aqueduct, which transports the water without pumping. Work began on 5 October 1921 with the Lord Mayor, Alderman A. Gadie, who cut the first sod. During the 15-year-long construction of the reservoir an entire village was constructed just below the dam to house the workforce. The population reached 2,000 and the village had all the amenities they might need. There were ten large hostels for workmen, 34 semi-detached bungalows, and 28 houses in five blocks. In 1926 the Scar Village Notes Newspaper wrote *'a smile will always do more than a frown, either in Scar Village or Harrogate Town'*, a sentiment that holds true today we would say.

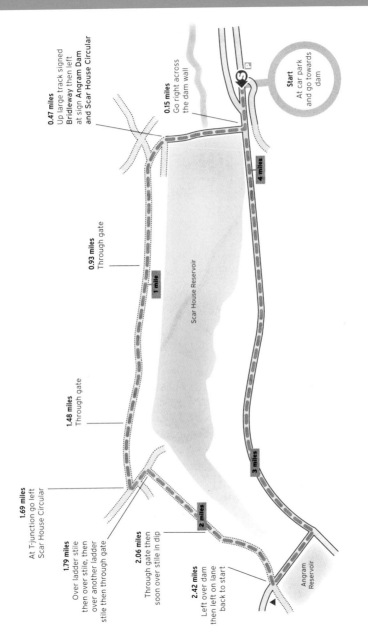

0.47 miles
Up large track signed
Bridleway then left
at sign **Angram Dam**
and **Scar House Circular**

0.15 miles
Go right across
the dam wall

Start
At car park
and go towards
dam

4 miles

0.93 miles
Through gate

1 mile

Scar House Reservoir

1.48 miles
Through gate

1.69 miles
At T-junction go left
Scar House Circular

1.79 miles
Over ladder stile
then over stile, then
over another ladder
stile then through gate

2.06 miles
Through gate then
soon over stile in dip

2 miles

2.42 miles
Left over dam
then left on lane
back to start

3 miles

Angram
Reservoir

31 Brideshead Visited

Lovely easy running around the Castle Howard Estate

Distance: **4.98 miles/8.01 km** | **Undulating** | EASY

Flat equiv.: **5.2 miles/8.37 km** | Climb rate: **12m/mile**

Terrain: **Road and trail**

Parking: **Free parking at Castle Howard**

Post code: **Y060 7DA** | Grid Ref: **SE 709699**

Start: **North from obelisk roundabout**

Brideshead was revisited in Evelyn Waugh's magnum opus, but we are content here with a single visit, looping around Castle Howard at a respectful distance.

This run is easy to follow around the Castle Howard Estate, where you can enjoy free views not only of the House but also of the many garden features and follies. Virtually everything has been altered on the estate – the hills, rivers and lakes – to create what the 18th century writers called 'the perfect landskip', based on Italian paintings and littered with classical buildings.

Facilities and safety

There is free parking at the Castle Howard car park, and free access to the coffee shop, toilets and shops in the stable block courtyard. The first mile and last short stretch is on a road so take care, though you can run on the wide verge if you prefer. The trails which make up half the run are well maintained and very good underfoot.

Interesting information

Castle Howard has been the seat of the Howard Family continuously for 300 years but is probably most famous for being the spectacular location used in the 1981 television adaptation of Evelyn Waugh's *Brideshead Revisited*, which starred Diana Rigg, Jeremy Irons and Anthony Andrews. Lonely Planet's *1,000 Ultimate Sights* promotes the Grade I listed mansion as: 'One of the World's Top Ten Greatest Mansions and Grand Houses'. So there, it must be worth a visit!

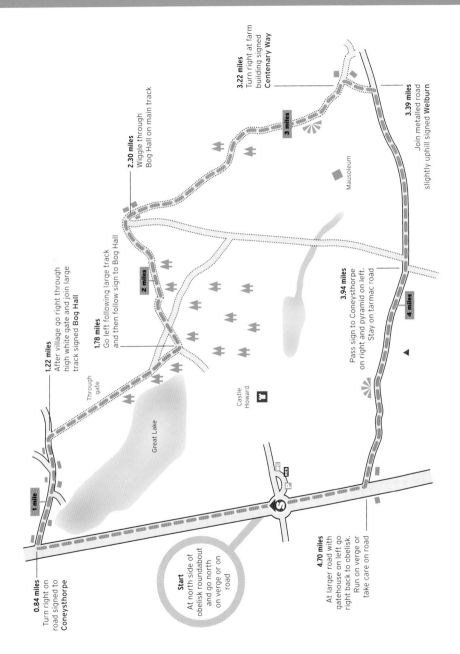

3.22 miles
Turn right at farm building signed **Centenary Way**

3.39 miles
Join metalled road slightly uphill signed **Welburn**

3 miles

Mausoleum

2.30 miles
Wiggle through Bog Hall on main track

2 miles

1.78 miles
Go left following large track and then follow sign to Bog Hall

3.94 miles
Pass sign to Coneysthorpe on right and pyramid on left. Stay on tarmac road

4 miles

1.22 miles
After village go right through high white gate and join large track signed **Bog Hall**

Through gate

Castle Howard

Great Lake

1 mile

0.84 miles
Turn right on road signed to **Coneysthorpe**

Start
At north side of obelisk roundabout and go north on verge or on road

4.70 miles
At larger road with gatehouse on left go right back to obelisk. Run on verge or take care on road

32 **The Devil's Hole**

The North Yorkshire Moors and its steam railway

Distance: **7.00 miles/11.26 km** | Hilly | **HARD**

Flat equiv.: **7.77 miles/12.50 km** | Climb rate: **29m/mile**

Terrain: **Trail and cross country**

Parking: **Free parking on the A169**

Post code: **YO18 7NR** | Grid Ref: **SE 852936**

Start: **Over the road, opposite the car park**

This is a devil of a route over the North Yorkshire Moors.

Wholly off road, the route first descends into and crosses the Hole of Horcum, before climbing up and crossing over Levisham Moor to arrive at Skelton Tower and the fantastic views down into the steep gorge of Newton Dale.

Facilities and safety

The start is over the road from the free car park south of Saltergate on the A169. There is usually a refreshment/ice cream van at the car park but there are no toilets. Take care descending into the Hole and along the edge of the gorge, especially along Huggitt's Scar and Yewtree Scar where the path is uneven. There is an alternative to this edge path – marked on the map at 4.58 miles. Also, after about 1.5 miles there is a narrow section which can get very muddy and slippery – bear with it as it is soon over.

Interesting information

The Hole was created when a giant named Wade, who was in fact a Saxon chief, grabbed a 'handful' of earth to throw at his wife, Bell. The soil missed its target and landed to form the 800-foot high hill of Blakey Topping about a mile to the east ... or it may have been the action over millennia of springs and rainwater. You decide for yourself!

The North Yorkshire Moors Railway passes along the gorge stopping at Newton Dale Halt on request. The steam trains run most of the year so if you are lucky you will first hear, and then see them passing along the gorge below you.

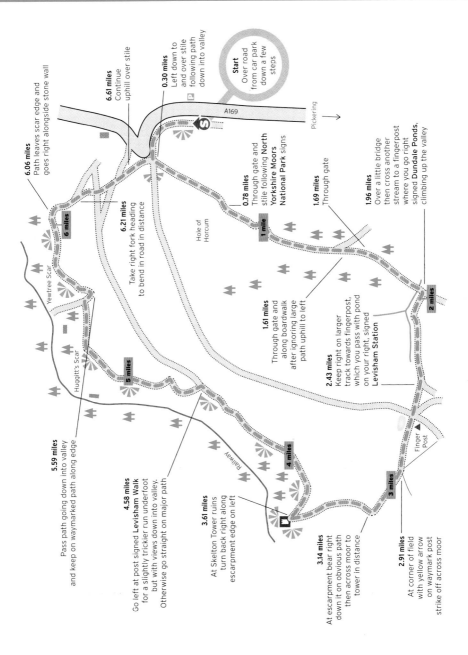

Start
Over road from car park down a few steps

0.30 miles
Left down to and over stile following path down into valley

6.61 miles
Continue uphill over stile

6.06 miles
Path leaves scar edge and goes right alongside stone wall

A169

Pickering →

Hole of Horcum

0.78 miles
Through gate and stile following **North Yorkshire Moors National Park** signs

1.69 miles
Through gate

1.96 miles
Over a little bridge then cross another stream to a fingerpost where you go right signed **Dundale Ponds**, climbing up the valley

6.21 miles
Take right fork heading to bend in road in distance

1 mile

Yewtree Scar

6 miles

1.61 miles
Through gate and along boardwalk after ignoring large path uphill to left

2 miles

2.43 miles
Keep right on larger track towards fingerpost, which you pass with pond on your right, signed **Levisham Station**

Huggitt's Scar

5 miles

5.59 miles
Pass path going down into valley and keep on waymarked path along edge

4.58 miles
Go left at post signed **Levisham Walk** for a slightly trickier run underfoot but with views down into valley. Otherwise go straight on major path

Railway

4 miles

Finger Post

3 miles

3.61 miles
At Skelton Tower ruins turn back right along escarpment edge on left

3.14 miles
At escarpment bear right down it on obvious path then across moor to tower in distance

2.91 miles
At corner of field with yellow arrow on waymark post strike off across moor

33 Robin Hood's Bay

Sumptuous views from coastal and railway paths

Distance: **4.70 miles/7.56 km** | Hilly | **MODERATE**

Flat equiv.: **5.17 miles/8.32 km** | Climb rate: **26m/mile**

Terrain: **Grassy coastal path and gravel trail**

Parking: **Pay and display on road into Robin Hood's Bay**

Post code: **YO22 4RE** | Grid Ref: **NZ 951054**

Start: **Over the road, opposite Grosvenor Hotel**

This is a pretty run along the coast north of the picturesque fishing village of Robin Hood's Bay.

Easy to follow in either direction, the run makes use of the scenic coastal path, the Cleveland Way and easy running cinder track, the railway path which is connected by a new path, the National Trust's Millennium Path. The coastal views are spectacular, especially down to pictuesque Robin Hood's Bay itself.

Facilities and safety

The pay and display parking (free in winter) is as you enter Robin Hood's Bay on the B1447 signed opposite the Grosvenor Hotel. There are toilets in the car park, and refreshments in the village and near the car park. There are no major safety concerns, simply mind the cliff path, which can be slippery, and the cyclists on the railway path. If you run the route clockwise, following the railway path first then back along the coast, don't miss the right turn – if you reach a road you have gone too far.

Interesting information

Robin Hood's Bay was famously the haunt of smugglers but no one knows why it is so named. One story says Robin was offered a pardon by the Abbot of Whitby for getting rid of North Yorkshire's pirates, another that he escaped the authorities here garbed as a local sailor. Pick your own tale or make one up as you see fit.

Early on in the run is a replica of a rocket post by which sailors on stricken ships were rescued by breeches buoy, which is more descriptive of the method than at first you might think!

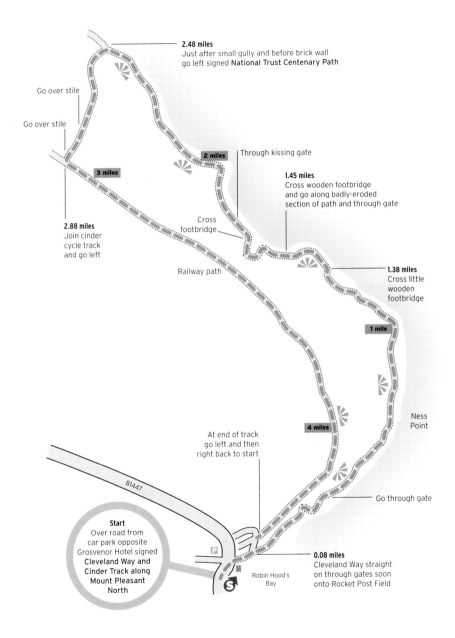

2.48 miles
Just after small gully and before brick wall
go left signed **National Trust Centenary Path**

Go over stile

Go over stile

3 miles

2 miles

Through kissing gate

1.45 miles
Cross wooden footbridge
and go along badly-eroded
section of path and through gate

2.88 miles
Join cinder
cycle track
and go left

Cross
footbridge

Railway path

1.38 miles
Cross little
wooden
footbridge

1 mile

4 miles

Ness
Point

At end of track
go left and then
right back to start

Go through gate

B1447

Start
Over road from
car park opposite
Grosvenor Hotel signed
Cleveland Way and
Cinder Track along
**Mount Pleasant
North**

Robin Hood's
Bay

0.08 miles
Cleveland Way straight
on through gates soon
onto Rocket Post Field

34 Wander Wordsworth's Lakes

Two homes, two lakes, a fell and a village

Distance: **7.15 miles/11.50 km** | Hilly | **EXTREME**

Flat equiv.: **8.50 miles/13.68 km** | Climb rate: **50m/mile**

Terrain: **Trail, fell and lane**

Parking: **Car park, southern end of Grasmere village**

Post code: **LA22 9SJ** | Grid Ref: **NY 339072**

Start: **Car park, Grasmere village**

William Wordsworth famously wandered the Lake District *'lonely as a cloud'* **and described Grasmere as the** *'loveliest spot that man hath ever found'.*

These days there is little chance of being lonely anywhere in the Lakes, yet it is still rather lovely as this run ably demonstrates. As you may have guessed this run has a strong William Wordsworth theme and passes through much of his favourite countryside and by two of his homes. It combines reasonably flat lakeside paths with rougher, higher paths giving great views over Rydal Water, Grasmere and Grasmere village.

Facilities and safety

Parking is available in the car park at the start, at the southern end of the village. There is a multitude of coffee shops, restaurants and pubs in the village, and the churchyard with Wordsworth's grave is very close to the start. An alternative start point, useful in high season when Grasmere gets very crowded, is the car park at the western end of Rydal Water.

The first part of this run is on road, followed by easy running around Rydal Water until some very steep climbing on rough trails. The final descent is on steep and rocky but well-defined paths.

Interesting information

This run passes Dove Cottage, the home of Wordsworth from 1799 to 1808 and Rydal Mount, his home from 1813 until his death in 1850. Also on the route one of his favourite watering holes – the Swan Hotel – used to charge his creative juices. Apparently, while staying with a friend he took the dog out for 'long walks' in the evening. One day he and his friend popped in to the Swan for some refreshment to be greeted by the barman *'Hello Mr Wordsworth, not got the dog with you today?'*

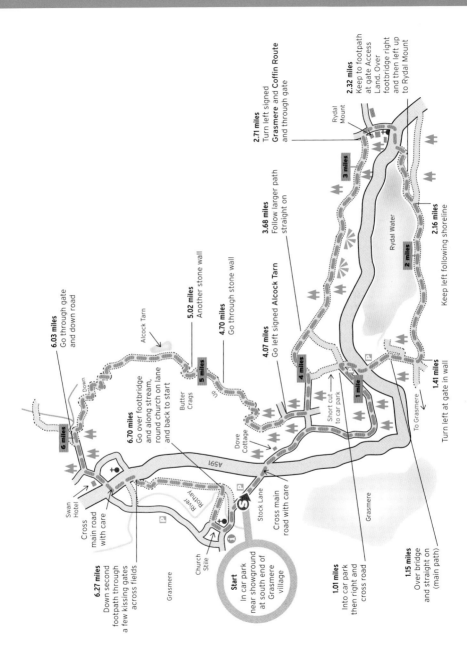

6.03 miles
Go through gate
and down road

Alcock Tarn

5.02 miles
Another stone wall

4.70 miles
Go through stone wall

6.70 miles
Go over footbridge
and along stream,
round church on lane
and back to start

Butter
Crags

Up

Down

5 miles

2.71 miles
Turn left signed
Grasmere and **Coffin Route**
and through gate

Rydal
Mount

2.32 miles
Keep to footpath
at gate Access
Land. Over
footbridge right
and then left up
to Rydal Mount

3 miles

3.68 miles
Follow larger path
straight on

Rydal Water

2 miles

2.16 miles

Keep left following shoreline

4.07 miles
Go left signed **Alcock Tarn**

4 miles

Short cut
to car park

1 mile

Dove
Cottage

A591

6 miles

Swan
Hotel

Cross
main road
with care

6.27 miles
Down second
footpath through
a few kissing gates
across fields

Grasmere

Church
Stile

River
Rothay

Stock Lane

Cross
main
road with care

Start
In car park
near showground
at south end of
Grasmere
village

1.01 miles
Into car park
then right and
cross road

Grasmere

To Grasmere

1.41 miles
Turn left at gate in wall

1.15 miles
Over bridge
and straight on
(main path)

WANDER WORDSWORTH'S LAKES

35 Dodd Hill

A tough climb to stunning Lakeland views

Distance: **4.2 miles/6.79 km** | Extreme | **EXTREME**

Flat equiv.: **5.48 miles/8.82 km** | Climb rate: **80m/mile**

Terrain: **Good gravel trail**

Parking: **Pay and display car park, A591 north of Keswick**

Post code: **CA12 4QE** | Grid Ref: **NY 235281**

Start: **Follow Osprey viewpoint signs from car park**

This tough trail route features good tracks throughout with spectacular views as you wind around Dodd forest and hill, with an optional (don't miss it!) lung-busting ascent to Dodd summit.

Note that although the tracks are good underfoot and well maintained, the amount of climbing is significant. This is in fact the steepest run of the 40 in this book.

Facilities and safety

There is pay and display parking at the start where you will also find the Old Sawmill cafe, information centre and toilets. Across the road is the historic Mirehouse – the gardens, playgrounds, lakeside walk and tearoom open daily from the end of March until the end of October. There are no roads to cross and no stiles en route, just lots of ascent and descent.

Interesting information

Thornthwaite Forest is a mish-mash of cultivated conifers and native self-seeded deciduous woodland, lying on a bed of Skiddaw slate. The area around the summit has been cleared so the views are superb, as are those on the climb. Skiddaw itself lies north east of the forest, an impressive 931 metres high, behind the slopes of Carl Side, equally impressive at 746 metres. Dodd Hill is a measly 502 metres by comparison. And of course watch out for the Bassenthwaite Ospreys overhead ...

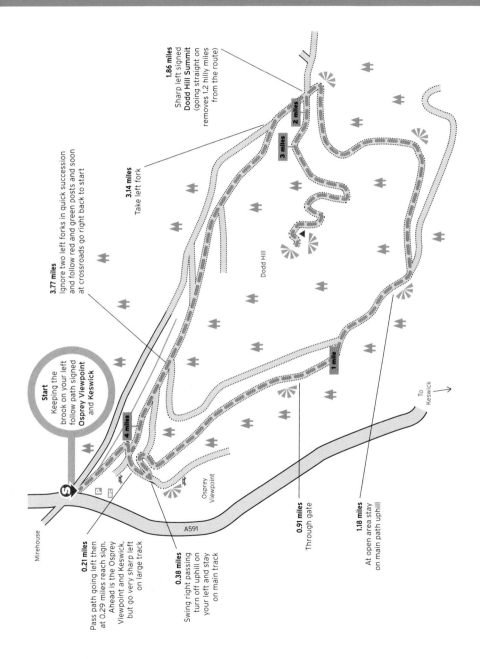

1.86 miles
Sharp left signed
Dodd Hill Summit
(going straight on
removes 1.2 hilly miles
from the route)

2 miles

3 miles

3.14 miles
Take left fork

Dodd Hill

3.77 miles
Ignore two left forks in quick succession
and follow red and green posts and soon
at crossroads go right back to start

Start
Keeping the
brook on your left
follow path signed
Osprey Viewpoint
and **Keswick**

4 miles

S

1 mile

To
Keswick

Osprey
Viewpoint

A591

Mirehouse

0.21 miles
Pass path going left then
at 0.29 miles reach sign.
Ahead is the Osprey
Viewpoint and Keswick,
but go very sharp left
on large track

0.38 miles
Swing right passing
turn off uphill on
your left and stay
on main track

0.91 miles
Through gate

1.18 miles
At open area stay
on main path uphill

36 Bassenthwaite Lake

Meander around little visited Lakeland paths

Distance: **7 miles/11.26 km** | **Hilly** | **HARD**

Flat equiv.: **8.1 miles/13.03 km** | Climb rate: **42m/mile**

Terrain: **Gravel trail, grassy tracks and short stretch of lane**

Parking: **Small car park at Beck Wythop, west of A66, north of Keswick**

Post code: **CA12 5SL** | Grid Ref: **NY 214284**

Start: **Up lane from car park on cycleway 71**

This is a run with bags of variety around Sale Fell and King's Wood on good trails.

The run starts with a stiff climb through a forest before venturing out onto and around the fell on good paths, finishing with a saunter along forest paths with great views of Bassenthwaite Lake and across to Skiddaw Fell.

Facilities and safety

The start is at a small parking area at Beck Wythop left off the A66, going north, immediately after it becomes a dual carriageway and soon after passing turns to Thornthwaite. There are no facilities at the parking area or on the route. There is a short road section with no footpath so take care even though you are unlikely to see any traffic. Much of the route is on forest trails, however, with some lovely grass paths across Sale Fell.

Interesting information

Bassenthwaite Lake holds the distinction of being the only lake in Lakeland, all the other large ones being named Water or Mere and the smaller, generally mountain lakes called Tarns. Thornthwaite Lodge, a local bed and breakfast, has a 'runner's corner' with many suggested runs as well as the usual walks. This run is one of them and to date the fastest time is just 40 minutes – not bad for seven tough miles!

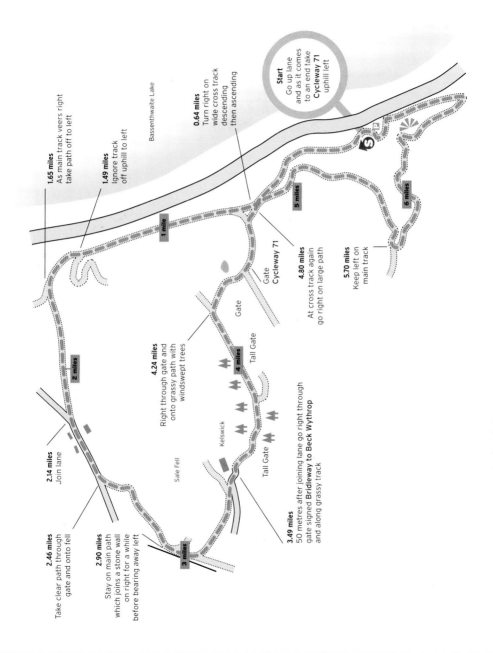

Start
Go up lane
and as it comes
to an end take
Cycleway 71
uphill left

0.64 miles
Turn right on
wide cross track
descending
then ascending

1.49 miles
Ignore track
off uphill to left

1.65 miles
As main track veers right
take path off to left

Bassenthwaite Lake

1 mile

5 miles

6 miles

5.70 miles
Keep left on
main track

4.80 miles
At cross track again
go right on large path

Gate
Cycleway 71

Gate

Tall Gate

4 miles

Tall Gate

4.24 miles
Right through gate and
onto grassy path with
windswept trees

Kelswick

Sale Fell

3.49 miles
50 metres after joining lane go right through
gate signed **Bridleway to Beck Wythrop**
and along grassy track

2 miles

2.14 miles
Join lane

2.46 miles
Take clear path through
gate and onto fell

2.90 miles
Stay on main path
which joins a stone wall
on right for a while
before bearing away left

3 miles

37 Hadrian's Wall Humdinger

The Roman Wall from within and without

Distance: **4.81 miles/7.74 km** | Hilly | **HARD**

Flat equiv.: **5.25 miles/8.45 km** | Climb rate: **25m/mile**

Terrain: **Stony trails and cross country**

Parking: **Steel Rigg car park, Bardon Mill, near Once Brewed**

Post code: **NE47 7AW** | Grid Ref: **NY 750676**

Start: **East on Hadrian's Wall Path, below car park**

This is a route with not only beautiful views but also bags of obvious historical interest.
The path along Hadrian's Wall has the history but is also tough going, with tricky and stony climbs and descents. The return path is across easier terrain and with a 'Picts' eye view of the formidable ancient fortification/border control.

Facilities and safety
Parking is pay and display at Steel Rigg car park, with the visitor centre down on the B6318 at the village of Twice Brewed. Please take care on the stony/paved descents and ascents along the wall path, which can be especially tricky and treacherous after rain. There is an alternative easier but less spectacular path south of the wall marked on the map.

Interesting information
Hadrian's Wall was built in AD 122 by order of Emperor Hadrian. It took three legions, each with about 15,000 men, just over six years to build. It is 73 miles (or 80 Roman miles) long and is the largest ancient monument in northern Europe. Impressive even today, it was once up to 20 feet high and 20 feet thick at its tallest and widest points.

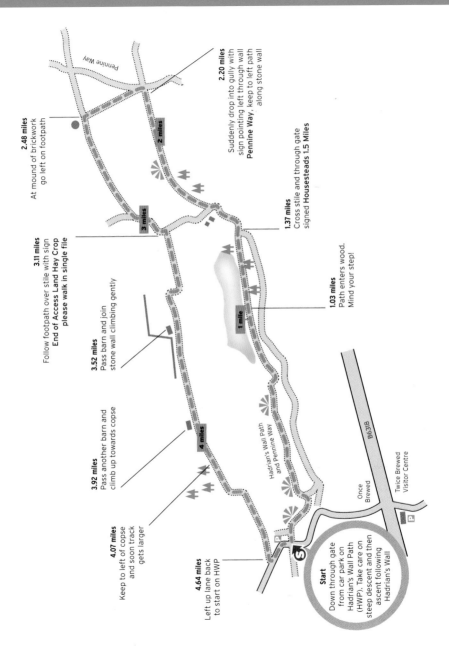

Pennine Way

2.48 miles
At mound of brickwork
go left on footpath

2.20 miles
Suddenly drop into gully with
sign pointing left through wall
Pennine Way, keep to left path
along stone wall

1.37 miles
Cross stile and through gate
signed **Housesteads 1.5 Miles**

2 miles

3 miles

3.11 miles
Follow footpath over stile with sign
End of Access Land Hay Crop
please walk in single file

3.52 miles
Pass barn and join
stone wall climbing gently

1.03 miles
Path enters wood.
Mind your step!

1 mile

3.92 miles
Pass another barn and
climb up towards copse

4 miles

4.07 miles
Keep to left of copse
and soon track
gets larger

Hadrian's Wall Path
and Pennine Way

B6318

Once
Brewed

Twice Brewed
Visitor Centre

4.64 miles
Left up lane back
to start on HWP

Start
Down through gate
from car park on
Hadrian's Wall Path
(HWP). Take care on
steep descent and then
ascent following
Hadrian's Wall

HADRIAN'S WALL HUMDINGER

38 **Simonside Summit**

Expansive views over Northumberland

Distance: **5 miles/8.04 km** | **Hilly** | **HARD**

Flat equiv.: **5.82 miles/9.36 km** | Climb rate: **44m/mile**

Terrain: **Road, gravel trail and stone path**

Parking: **Lordenshaw car park, off the B6342 south of Rothbury**

Post code: **NE61 4PU** | Grid Ref: **NZ 052987**

Start: **Right along lane from car park**

To see this route at its best a nice dry autumn day would be ideal. The route reaches a height of 429 metres at the summit of Simonside.

From here you will see many of the great views of Northumberland, with the Cheviots away to the north and Fontburn reservoir to the south and on a clear day the line of the coast can clearly be followed.

Facilities and safety

Lordenshaw car park is free, but there are no amenities. The forest car park at the one mile mark is also free and has a small picnic area. The route itself starts along a lane and then onto generally good tracks with only a few slightly testing rocky sections. The descent is mostly on a paved path with again only a few testing sections to take care on. This flag-stoned path, laid in 2010 over the boggy plateau of the Simonside Hills, is part of the erosion control measures to allow recovery of the original eroded route on the northern edge which is now closed.

Despite being quite a high level route the underfoot conditions are generally good and the slopes not too steep. Take care on the quiet lane and on the rocky path especially in the wet. It's not too difficult a route but in inclement weather it would be advisable to take a map, compass, food, drink and full body cover.

Interesting information

The area is very popular with walkers, the path up to the summit being dry and well cared for, especially compared to the very boggy St Oswald's Way that crosses the moor, so on a fine day you'll have plenty of company.

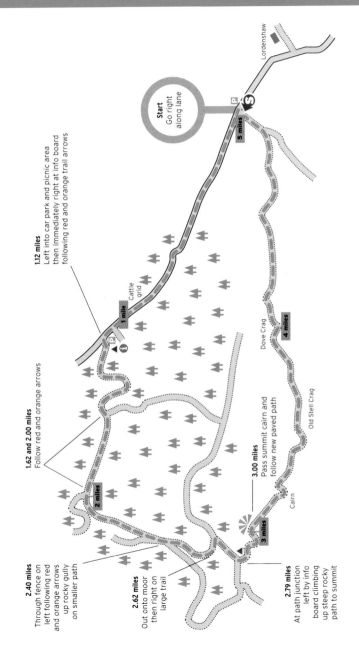

Lordenshaw

Start
Go right
along lane

5 miles

1.12 miles
Left into car park and picnic area
then immediately right at info board
following red and orange trail arrows

1 mile Cattle
grid

1.62 and 2.00 miles
Follow red and orange arrows

Dove Crag

4 miles

2 miles

Old Stell Crag

3.00 miles
Pass summit cairn and
follow new paved path

2.40 miles
Through fence on
left following red
and orange arrows
up rocky gully
on smaller path

Cairn

3 miles

2.62 miles
Out onto moor
then right on
large trail

2.79 miles
At path junction
left by info
board climbing
up steep rocky
path to summit

39 Dunstanburgh Castle Canter

The beautiful ruined castle from almost every angle

Distance: **4.83 miles/7.77 km** | **Undulating** | EASY

Flat equiv.: **5.06 miles/8.14 km** | Climb rate: **13m/mile**

Terrain: **Coast path, concrete lane and cross country**

Parking: **Craster car park**

Post code: **NE66 3TW** | Grid Ref: **NU 257199**

Start: **Path towards Craster from car park**

The Northumberland coast is noted for its many picturesque castles dotted along its rugged coastline. Dunstanburgh Castle, though, is perhaps the most iconic.

A romantic Grade I listed ruin on its own headland, it can be seen jutting out into the sea for many miles from either direction. Adding to its charm is the fact it can only be reached on foot either from Craster village, one mile south, or a remote car park about one mile north. This run features a wide range of challenges – grassy exposed coastal path (mind the wind!), sand dunes, concrete bridleway and a few gates and stiles. Running the route in the other direction renders the picturesque castle from an equally pleasing aspect, or you could cut back the other side of the golf course for an alternative route.

Facilities and safety

There's pay and display parking in Craster, and free parking at the halfway point. There are toilets in the car park, and the Jolly Fisherman Pub in the village. A visitor centre is only open at weekends. Mind the wind off the North Sea and some sections can be a little slippery underfoot.

Interesting information

Earl Thomas of Lancaster started the construction of the grand castle in 1313 but it was the Wars of the Roses that started the decay. The castle was held for the Lancastrians in 1462 and 1464 but the damage was not made good and the castle fell steadily into decay. A report in 1550 described it as in *'wonderfull great decaye'*. The castle was painted by the British Romantic painter J. M. W. Turner numerous times. One of his oil paintings of Dunstanburgh can be found in the Dunedin Public Art Gallery in New Zealand.

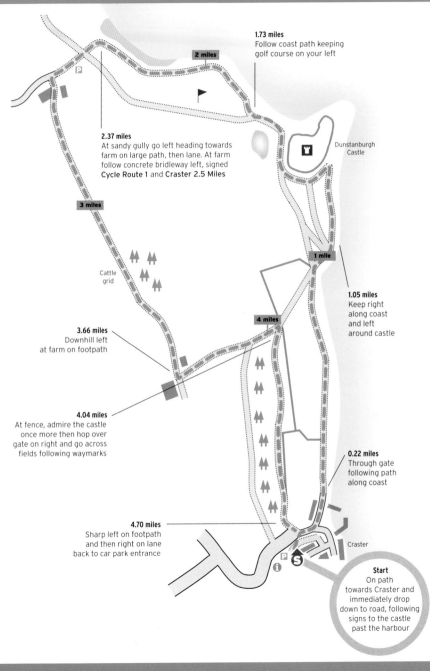

1.73 miles
Follow coast path keeping
golf course on your left

2 miles

2.37 miles
At sandy gully go left heading towards
farm on large path, then lane. At farm
follow concrete bridleway left, signed
Cycle Route 1 and **Craster 2.5 Miles**

Dunstanburgh
Castle

3 miles

Cattle
grid

1 mile

1.05 miles
Keep right
along coast
and left
around castle

3.66 miles
Downhill left
at farm on footpath

4 miles

4.04 miles
At fence, admire the castle
once more then hop over
gate on right and go across
fields following waymarks

0.22 miles
Through gate
following path
along coast

4.70 miles
Sharp left on footpath
and then right on lane
back to car park entrance

Craster

Start
On path
towards Craster and
immediately drop
down to road, following
signs to the castle
past the harbour

40 Bamburgh Castle Bumble

Countryside, coast and a castle

Distance: **5.49 miles/8.84 km** | **Undulating** | **MODERATE**

Flat equiv.: **5.77 miles/9.29 km** | Climb rate: **14m/mile**

Terrain: **Road, cross country and sandy coastal path**

Parking: **Bamburgh Castle pay and display or free roadside parking in Bamburgh village**

Post code: **NE69 7DF** | Grid Ref: **NU 183349**

Start: **West past castle and fork right in Bamburgh**

This varied and beautiful run is centred on the picturesque Bamburgh Castle. This run features pretty countryside, quiet lanes, stunning rugged coastline and the iconic castle.
   The course is gently undulating with just a few stiles to hop over, gorgeous countryside, a lovely run along the coast path and of course views of the stunning castle.

Facilities and safety

There is pay and display parking at Bamburgh Castle but parking is free around the triangle in the centre of the village where there are also toilets. Take care on the roads where some sections have no footpaths, where especially in the summer you will have plenty of walkers to keep you company. There are numerous cafes, pubs, and shops around the triangle in the centre of Bamburgh.

Interesting information

The imposing castle at Bamburgh is perched on a basalt outcrop and was probably first used as a fortification in the 5th century AD. In the 11th century the Normans rebuilt the castle, much of which endures to this day. In the distance you can see both Lindisfarne Castle and the Farne Islands. The Farne Islands are noted for their wildlife including puffins, terns and grey seals. The village of Seahouses, three miles to the south of Bamburgh, has a thriving business taking tourists to the islands for bird watching and diving.

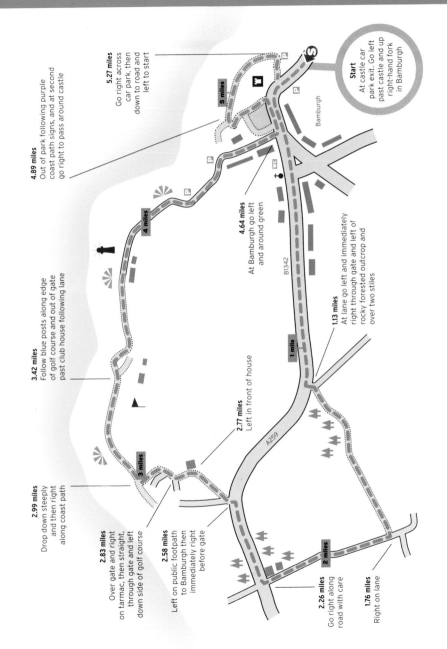

Start
At castle car park exit. Go left past castle and up right-hand fork in Bamburgh

5.27 miles
Go right across car park, then down to road and left to start

4.89 miles
Out of park following purple coast path signs, and at second go right to pass around castle

5 miles

3.42 miles
Follow blue posts along edge of golf course and out of gate past club house following lane

4 miles

4.64 miles
At Bamburgh go left and around green

1.13 miles
At lane go left and immediately right through gate and left of rocky forested outcrop and over two stiles

Bamburgh

B1342

1 mile

2.77 miles
Left in front of house

2.99 miles
Drop down steeply and then right along coast path

A259

3 miles

2.83 miles
Over gate and right on tarmac, then straight, through gate and left down side of golf course

2.58 miles
Left on public footpath to Bamburgh then immediately right before gate

2 miles

2.26 miles
Go right along road with care

1.76 miles
Right on lane

WE PUBLISH A WIDE RANGE OF AWARD WINNING BOOKS, FOR MOUNTAIN BIKERS, CYCLISTS, RUNNERS, HILL WALKERS, CLIMBERS AND MOUNTAINEERS.

HERE'S A FEW OF OUR BOOKS:

ADVENTURES IN MIND
Why do we do it? In her first book, leading fell runner, adventure racer and cyclist Heather Dawe writes a fast-paced and intensely personal examination of what drives her – and others – to push themselves in the great outdoors.

GREAT BRITAIN MOUNTAIN BIKING
A comprehensive area-by-area guide to the best mountain biking in England, Scotland and Wales. Tom Fenton and Andy McCandlish have compiled everything you need to know about Britain's top riding spots in this ideal companion for planning weekends away.

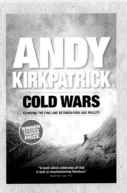

COLD WARS
In the brilliant sequel to his award-winning debut book *Psychovertical*, mountaineering stand-up Andy Kirkpatrick has achieved his life's ambition to become one of the world's leading climbers. Pushing himself to new extremes, he embarks on his toughest climbs yet – on big walls in the Alps and Patagonia – in the depths of winter. Winner of the Boardman Tasker Prize.

GREAT BRITISH BIKE RIDES
Dave Barter brings together 40 of the best road rides in England, Scotland and Wales, searching out the country's most celebrated routes, toughest climbs and most scenic roads.

Good Run Guide

**THE UK'S LEADING
INDEPENDENT
RUNNING WEBSITE:**
researching and
mapping the best
routes and providing
inspiration and
motivation for runners.

Visit us online for more fantastic routes
and for measuring and downloading your
UK and international routes, logging and
planning training, comprehensive graphs
and stats, good impartial running advice,
UK race listings and much more.

www.goodrunguide.co.uk